Pitt Series in Nature and Natural History

Jack Wennerstrom

Soldiers Delight Journal

Exploring a Globally Rare Ecosystem

Foreword by Roger Tory Peterson
Illustrations by Sandy Glover

University of Pittsburgh Press • Pittsburgh and London

Published by the University of Pittsburgh Press, Pittsburgh, Pa. 15260

Manufactured in the United States of America
Printed on acid-free paper

LIBRARY OF CONGRESS CATALOGING-IN-PUBLICATION DATA
Wennerstrom, Jack, 1948–
    Soldiers Delight journal : exploring a globally rare ecosystem /
Jack Wennerstrom ; foreword by Roger Tory Peterson
        p.   cm. — (Pittsburgh series in nature and natural history)
    Includes bibliographical references (p.   ) and index.
    ISBN 0-8229-3870-7 (cl).—ISBN 0-8229-5550-4 (pb)
    1. Natural history—Maryland—Soldiers Delight Natural Environment Area.
    2. Wennerstrom, Jack, 1948—Diaries.   3. Soldiers Delight Natural
Environment
Area (Md.)   I. Title.   II. Series.
    QH105.M3W45   1994
    508.752'71—dc20   94-41302
                          CIP

A CIP catalogue record for this book is available from the British Library.
Eurospan, London

I wish to thank the following people for their kind support: Rodney Bartgis, Fraser Bishop, Gene Cooley, Jim Flater, Peter Jayne, Johnny Johnsson, Sue May, Pat Milner, Clyde Reed, Dick Smith, Warren Steiner, Sara Tangren, Wayne Tyndall, Dave Walbeck, and Jean Worthley.

To Donna, who made it all possible

An eye that can see Nature,
A heart that can feel Nature,
A will that can follow Nature.

The three conditions required by
"awen," or "the creative inspiration,"
as enunciated by an ancient Celtic bard.

To find new things, take the path
you took yesterday.

—*John Burroughs*

Contents

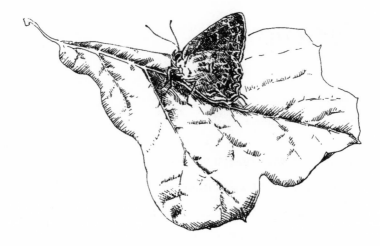

Foreword

We live in a world of shrinking wild places. While human interest in the natural world seems to be constantly growing, our burgeoning global population makes it inevitable that this interest will be focused on fewer and fewer wild acres.

The wild serpentine grasslands of eastern North America were once extensive but never truly vast. They have now shrunk to mere fragments. Worldwide, pockets of serpentine rock and soil comprise less than 1 percent of the earth's land mass, in beautiful, bizarre, or haunting places—in Quebec, Scotland, and Sweden; in Spain, Italy, and Bosnia; in Africa, Australia, and Malaysia; in Brazil, California, and Oregon. Each has its own individual biota, a biota now threatened by man, who both overvalues his own importance and undervalues the natural environment.

It was to raise the profile of such places, and to savor their special beauty, that Jack Wennerstrom wrote this book.

He also wrote it because he believes wild places, while shrinking, are more numerous than many think. There is, as he has said, "a natural door to solitude near almost every community." Soldiers Delight Natural Environment Area sits hard by the metro regions of Baltimore and Washington. Although unique in many ways, it is not so different from parks and preserves that border urban and suburban centers elsewhere and that may exist not too far from where we live.

The author, in his journal year, did not pursue just the rare or exotic; he deliberately sought out the everyday in nature, the abundant aliens as well as the familiar natives—the pheasants and chickadees, fungi and chicories, that are the stuff of everyone's adventures in the woods or fields not far from home, wherever they live.

Living in the country halfway between New York and Boston, near the mouth of the Connecticut River, I was able to relate to Jack Wennerstrom's journal and will continue to keep a journal of my own.

ROGER TORY PETERSON

Introduction

Without the potential for discovery, life is unutterably dull. I tend to best realize this potential in nature. Even in the smallest park or natural area there is so much to learn, such beauty to uncover, such a broad array of tiny, half-hidden worlds, that perhaps the greatest discovery is of the extent to which these are usually overlooked.

My exploration of Soldiers Delight Natural Environment Area in Baltimore County, Maryland, while by no means my first intimate encounter with a single wild place, exceeded all others in degree, and surprised me with the hold it finally gained on my psyche. By the midpoint of my journal year, I began to feel stifled when more than a few days passed between visits there. Though random approach is not always a virtue, it now seems the very essence of my year's revelations. The excitement and satisfaction brought by serendipitous discoveries was great and seemed to build upon itself until I formed the kind of blissful addiction to observant wandering that Thoreau knew so well.

Both natural and human history were the objects of my scrutiny, though with clear emphasis on the former. I have tried to describe a representative number of intriguing flora and fauna, and have by no means attempted to list all of the area's species. Soldiers Delight is a globally rare natural community, and, in the interest of scientific accuracy, my original intention was to site both the common and Latin name of each species I mentioned. Like a literary briar patch, however, this caught too much at the narrative cloth, so in the text I have included Latin names for all species but those of birds and mammals, animal groups wherein the least confusion of identity exists.

But mine is a subjective account, not a scientific treatise. If science is the key to discovery, then emotion and feeling are the hands that turn it, for without a strong sense of beauty or wonder there is no motivation, and the key is but a lifeless tool. This interdependence of mind and spirit is crucial. The scientist can not succeed without inspiration, nor the poet without reason. I have here tried to strike an appropriate balance, however imperfect, and when dipping too low at one end, have thrown some weight toward the other.

Yet my true goal was not one of balance, but of grip. I hoped to get a handle on those imponderables that attend all closeness with the outdoors, to, now and again, hold up nature's glory for inspection and turn it in the light. There is a luster and resonance in wildness that is beyond form, beyond function. Each time one goes afield it is revealed that much more and stored up in the soul. It mostly defies translation, so few even bother to try. For a long time I didn't try either. But, if you're a writer, the need to attempt such translations gets under your skin. I finally got a notebook and jotted a few things down.

Soldiers Delight Journal

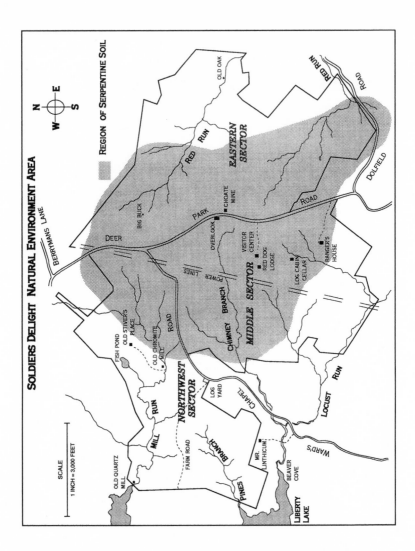

SOLDIERS DELIGHT NATURAL ENVIRONMENT AREA

SCALE
1 INCH = 3,000 FEET

N
W E
S

REGION OF SERPENTINE SOIL

BERRYMANS LANE

OLD OAK

RED RUN

ROAD

DOLFIELD

BIG BUCK

CHOATE MINE

DEER   PARK   ROAD

OVERLOOK

VISITOR CENTER

RED DOG LODGE

LOG CABIN CELLAR

RANGER'S HOUSE

EASTERN SECTOR

POWER LINES

CHIMNEY BRANCH

MIDDLE SECTOR

FISH POND

OLD STIVER'S PLACE

OLD CHROMITE MILL ROAD

MILL RUN

NORTHWEST SECTOR

LOG YARD

CHAPEL

FARM ROAD

BRANCH

MR. LINTHICUM

BEAVER COVE

WARD'S

LOCUST RUN

OLD QUARTZ MILL

PINES

LIBERTY LAKE

January *Companioned by All My Senses*

Red Crossbill

Reindeer Lichen

Winter Wren

January 1

There is a rare ecosystem just seven miles from the city boundary of Baltimore, Maryland. It is a unique area of prairie remnants and rocky soils that contains not only scarce habitats and their specialized plants, but a mix of other natural systems that even the experts overlook. It is called Soldiers Delight.

Some people think Soldiers Delight an underused region of parched grasslands and thin woods, scattered throughout with strange botanical specimens. Quite true, and very much a part of its charm. But it is also an area with extensive forests to the west, streams and ponds, overgrown pastures, farm fields, lush little floodplains and hidden valleys, and odd fragments of human history. And then there is Liberty Lake—a vast reservoir sheltering odd birds and mammals, and many species of fish—whose fingery easternmost coves are visible from the park in winter.

In the new year I have resolved to explore this place fully, to make it my natural home. I am lucky in not having far to go. It is a place nearby.

January 2

I brushed up on some Soldiers Delight history today. About twenty-five thousand years ago, the climate here was warmer and drier, and the region was covered by a vast prairielike grassland. Most of central Maryland and southeastern Pennsylvania formed the heart of these arid prairies, where stunted oaks—in open formations known as savannas—comprised the few woody plants. Hardwood forests encroached as the climate grew wetter and cooler, but native peoples, who burned the grasslands in hunting, helped preserve them. The prairies were further protected by a band of metamorphic rock called serpentinite that still stretches from Quebec to Alabama. Soil eroded from outcrops of serpentinite—the so-called serpentine soil—is shallow, dry, nutrient poor, and high in plant-toxic minerals such as magnesite, chromite, and iron oxide. Over centuries, unique plants adapted themselves to this harsh environment, which continued to be eroded by climatic change and forest transition, and, most recently, by the displacement of both tribal peoples and large grazing mammals. Finally, the agricultural and mining disturbances brought by immigrant Europeans in the last two centuries were especially destructive. The unproductive "dryness" of the rocky barrens was not enough to protect them from the uses and misuses of human beings.

Today only four major remnants of serpentine grassland remain in Maryland, less than 5 percent of the original area. Even these have been badly fragmented by the intrusion of pines, cedars, and other woody plants, leaving small "glades" of prairie. Yet over thirty-five rare and endangered plant species still exist in the largest of these remnants—Soldiers Delight.

January 4

As I've done so often, I drove along the two main roads through Soldiers Delight—Deer Park and Ward's Chapel. They cut through the bleakest of the serpentine barrens, and, with the exception of the overlook off Deer Park, suggest little natural splendor. I stopped and walked my familiar circuit into the northeast corner and enjoyed the hardwood habitats beyond the prairie glades, down in the Red Run floodplain. The green of mountain laurel *(Kalmia latifolia)* on the hillsides there stands out against winter's gray and brown, and the streams, working under patches of ice, release hypnotic gurgles.

Meanwhile, a map that the ranger Fraser Bishop showed me grows ever more intriguing. In degree of detail it easily exceeds the U.S. Geological Survey map; everything from ditches and springs to boulders and old fences are charted. The whole northwest sector of Soldiers Delight is of oddly mixed habitats, and I'm anxious to probe them.

I don't mind exploring such places alone. In fact I rather prefer it, though I'm reluctant to admit this among my naturalist friends. They know me as a willing companion, a sharer of outdoor adventure. Yet I find my grasp of wild things is improved when I go solo.

When alone I feel more alert and somehow more resourceful. Stimuli strike in bunches, are digested more completely, and used to build fresh thought, new wonder. I say nothing foolish for there is no one there to listen. At such times "alone," in fact, is not quite what I am. I am companioned by all my senses, which fan out and search with me as though my private band of woodsmen, fanatically devoted. There is no need to plan a rendezvous, to debate which routes are best, or to set a time for lunch. They share my wants and opinions. When it is over we will all meet back at the house or car, simultaneously, with infallible precision.

Some years ago I led an assortment of affable adults on bird walks in central Maryland. We saw wonderful things. Yet I often felt distracted and emotionally removed. While walking those same places alone, however, the simplest natural encounters would enchant me. Once I followed a male summer tanager through mixed oak and pine till he linked up with his mate. His tolerance of me seemed odd. I toyed with the silly notion that he had *led* me to his female, for he surely knew I was following and could have steered me away. Words like "affinity" and "sympathetic bond" leaped to mind. This is dangerous ground for a naturalist. You must take care not to dip science too deeply in your vat of wonder.

Yet, tramping alone, I can indulge this harmless pleasure. Not everything that assails the mind can be dealt with in rational terms. I expect I will rediscover this on my treks through Soldiers Delight. Indeed, with the tanagers, during that brief encounter long ago, I felt near to inventing some myth about them and their link with mankind. Another hour with the pair, a cynic might suggest, and I'd have glimpsed my own clues to Creation, reinventing the universe through the behavior of a bird. I think of our native peoples and do not laugh. Not by accident were young men sent forth alone to find their spirit reflection among the birds and beasts.

January 8

There was wet snow in early morning, which coated every tree branch and twig in a lovely "flocked" effect. I hurried over to the sector off Ward's Chapel Road, parked, and walked northwest. The bare glades dropped down to a stream, and then the trail rose through edges and pastures into woods. The sun came out and broadcast the brilliance of the sky and snow-flocked trees. I just stopped in my tracks at one point, breathed the cold air deeply, listened to a Carolina chickadee in the bright stillness, and gazed spellbound at the whitened beauty all around. When I got up further into a grove between two fields, I heard a ring-necked pheasant croak, then another. Suddenly a big cock pheasant appeared in a tree overhead, his striking patterns and colors lit by the sunlight as he balanced himself amid snow-cottoned branches.

Normally pheasants are ground dwellers; they are too bulky and flamboyantly appointed to survive long in trees. Thus there was something jarring about this overhead cameo of Christmas-card beauty. It was pleasant but not quite real, even faintly ludicrous. As I walked on, two hens exploded from the brambles on my right, then a second cock, a third, and a fourth. I counted almost a dozen in the next quarter mile. Finally I approached a farmyard on my left where, through the timber, I spotted quail and chukar imprisoned in a pen. A dead cock pheasant at my feet, with a strange plastic ring through its beak, confirmed my suspicion that many of these birds were farm-bred escapes. A phone call, on my return, to Fraser Bishop, confirmed this and more. Yes, the man raises birds, said Fraser, and two thousand pheasants had escaped that morning when snow collapsed an enclosure. The surprise was not that I'd seen so many, but that I hadn't seen more.

January 9

Cloudy and windy. I explored the middle sector, an invert-ed V formed by the two main roads. Again I heard pheasants:

the male's loud *kuk-krok!* sounds, from a distance, like a small gas engine being cranked. Their tracks were everywhere in the thin snow. These I suspect were the older residents of the park, not new escapes, although the question is one of degree. Ring-necked pheasants are not native but were imported from China last century and released widely by sportsmen. So even the wildest stock has a lineage whose "wildness" is recent.

Northern juncos and white-throated sparrows were the most common native species today. Neither will nest here in summer; by May they'll head north for breeding. Of fifteen bird species this morning, a hermit thrush was the choicest. They are uncommon but consistent winter residents, quietly haunting the windless little pine groves and greenbriar tangles, graybrown and speckle-breasted, dipping their tawny tails. The hardiest and most solitary of the seven eastern thrush species, hermits can survive our coldest winters without help or handout from humans.

I stopped to see Fraser Bishop afterward. As the full-time ranger and area manager he is provided a house on the southern edge of the Soldiers Delight. We talked about rocks and minerals, and he asked me if I'd seen the local asbestos. I admitted I hadn't. He peered down to search his driveway. "It looks like petrified wood," he said. With this clue alone I joined him in hunting and quickly found an inch-long fragment at our feet. This was a piece of what is more precisely termed "picrolite," a harder, less flexible form of fibrous serpentinite, related to chrysotile asbestos, that has a lustrous green-gray color and a splintery, columnar grain. From a distance it is a dead ringer for wood, and the little shards and fractured hunks are common in some of the glades, inviting the eye with their odd shape and verdant sheen, especially after a rain.

January 14

In afternoon I wandered the northwest sector again. There is a small pond there, perhaps an acre overall. Yet it is the largest pond at Soldiers Delight. Fraser says it is stocked with bluegill and bass, which I'll try to confirm this summer.

I hiked south to a little stream valley, past a big maple tree that had been "step-fitted" with railroad spikes, allowing easy ascent to the deer stand in its fork. From such platforms local poachers hunt white-tailed deer in autumn. Fraser hunts the poachers.

Working back I crossed the creek and flushed a great blue heron from the brushy bank. I was quite near before he saw me, and his huge wingspan and coiled grace in rising thrilled me. As usual after such encounters I stopped instantly and sat down at the spot. It is then that I often make interesting further discoveries. Is it because the excitement of the moment lifts my senses, and opens them to greater awareness, or is it something more imponderable? I only know that I sat quietly at the sandy streamside for a bit, and found some rock and mineral fragments of pleasing purity and luster.

January 15

Soldiers Delight Natural Environment Area is about two thousand acres, or five square miles in area. I have come to view it as three regions: the northwest sector, west of Ward's

Chapel Road; the middle sector, in the V between Ward's Chapel and Deer Park Roads; and the eastern sector, east of Deer Park. The middle sector and the west end of the eastern sector contain the greatest percentage of serpentine grassland, for which Soldiers Delight is best noted.

The names serpentine and serpentinite are tied to the folklore of Italy, and, according to one theory, are derived from the surface pattern of the rock type, which resembles the markings of an Italian snake that lives in related terrain. In a similar context, the name may be traced back as far as Pliny the Elder, the first-century Roman naturalist, who called it "ophite," from the Greek word "ophis," meaning serpent. Pliny's contemporary, Dioscorides, a Greek physician who followed the Roman armies, claimed it prevented snakebite. Others of the time apparently used it when bitten, as a poultice, for certain serpentine minerals, such as the magnesium silicate "meerschaum," have a drawing effect on human tissue. Many Europeans still call serpentine ophite, or ophiolite.

Serpentine is a secondary mineral, the product of changes in igneous and metamorphic rock. Other, often unrelated, rocks and minerals, particularly dunite and peridotite, were gradually altered by a complex hydrothermal process known as serpentinization. The rock serpentinite is an ultramafic rock, that is, one containing less than 45 percent silica and more than 70 percent iron and magnesium minerals. Often comprised of the magnesium silicates antigorite and chrysotile, it is usually grayish green in color. But depending on which other minerals are present, it varies from yellowish to black. It is smooth and greasy to the touch, and, besides magnesium silicates, frequently contains chromite—which was mined here for most of a century—plus iron, nickel, cobalt, aluminum, talc, and additional minerals or chemical elements in lesser amounts.

Originally part of the mantle, that layer just below the earth's ten- to twenty-five mile thick crust, the area's serpentinite outcrops are the result of a geological dynamic that to this day is subject to some conjecture. A long series of complicated upliftings and movements, including lithospheric plate collision and spreading of the ancient seafloor, are the most likely explanations for its present emplacement as surface bedrock.

What *is* certain is that the Piedmont region in which Soldiers Delight exists is the most mineral rich in Maryland. While rock here is so highly metamorphosed that most fossils have not survived, the area is dense with crystalline formations, which are the basis of many gemstones.

This morning, among my streambed rock fragments from yesterday, I found unusually pretty samples of mica and picrolite. Such incidental rocks and minerals are some of the area's most fascinating. According to one local resident, mica was once briefly mined in sheets from a little known location at Soldiers Delight, and used to fashion such items as semi-transparent fireplace screens. Other rocks and minerals, like jasper, agate, garnet, geothite, and soapstone—which have weathered out of the serpentinite itself—can be found on the surface. Pick up a good size chunk of serpentinite in some areas of Soldiers Delight, and you may find its surface dotted with brownish facets of garnet crystal, dulled by rusted iron-oxide. Bits of black chrome fleck other hunks of serpentinite, in a form known as "bird's-eye" serpentine. Still other minerals have been discovered in mine shafts and diggings: rhodochrome, calcite, baltimorite (a picrolite common to

Baltimore's "Bare Hills" neighborhood), chalcedony (which includes carnelian, and the jaspers and agates), williamsite (a lovely pale green translucent serpentine), deweylite (which appears like bits of hardened toffee in some rocks), and spinel.

Spinel is rare and highly interesting. Composed mostly of aluminum oxide, it has a glassy luster and may be black, green, blue, red, violet, orange, or white, and anywhere from opaque to transparent, even fluorescent. At Soldiers Delight it has been found at the Weir Mine (as a blue black to dark green form known as pleonast), but some of its red forms are valuable as jewelry stones, and are often mistaken for rubies. In fact, one of Britain's Crown Jewels, the "Black Prince Ruby," is actually a red spinel.

January 19

I helped out with Bob Ringler's Midwinter Bird Count by birding Soldiers Delight in the morning, working the northwest sector entirely. Many people are familiar with the Christmas Bird Count, an attempt by bird-watchers, on a day during the Christmas season, to tally species and individuals in a given area, thus providing some record of bird numbers and distribution during one of the year's bleaker months. A few feel the count is misleading, especially because, in December, fall migration has not yet ended, while species incursions from the North and elsewhere—a nearly annual occurence—have not had time to develop. The Midwinter Bird Count, in late January, may correct this deficiency and provide a more accurate picture of bird populations in winter.

During my count at Soldiers Delight, I met a bow hunter

along the lake trail and we chatted as we walked. The bow season ends in two weeks. We both commented on the beauty of this wooded upland trail, where blue coves shown below us through the bare oaks and poplars.

Two red-breasted nuthatches and a great horned owl were my best birds until the finish, when I stopped to drink coffee in a pine grove near my car. As I unscrewed my thermos, sunlight played in the treetops, where reddish birds were flitting. Thinking them merely house or purple finches, I listlessly raised my lenses to find red orange males and greenish yellow females with dark wings and tails, feeding upside down on cones of Virginia pine *(Pinus virginiana)*. These were red crossbills, only my second lifetime sighting, and first ever in the East.

Crossbills are finchlike birds whose upper and lower mandibles (beak parts) overlap like crimp-ended scissors, forming a tool that easily cracks seeds, especially those of pine, which are the bird's principle food. There are but two North American species, and their normal southerly range skims the region of the northern Great Lakes. Yet crossbills are highly nomadic, often moving south in search of food, and their winter occurrence at Soldiers Delight, with its numerous stands of pine, has been noted several times in the past.

Red crossbills are acrobatic, noisy feeders, audibly snapping seed husks as they hang inverted in the shadows or sway on springy branches, their tanager tones half-concealed in the green, or lit by glints of sunshine. This morning I counted perhaps a dozen, occupied with feeding for several minutes before, when I tried to get closer, they set up a high-pitched din, rose in confusion, and came together in a tight pulsing bunch, tweaking madly toward the west.

January 22

A bright, frigid day—ten degrees above zero—with a strong west wind. I bundled up and explored the middle sector, starting from Fraser's driveway. Nearby is a large, almost impassable area of both common greenbriar *(Smilax rotundifolia)* and glaucous greenbriar *(Smilax glauca)*, just west of the power lines. I tried to penetrate from several angles without success, finally dropping down to Locust Run, and working in from the south. Here there are big outcrops of "trap rock" (a type of gabbro), covered with bright moss and lichens.

After many starts and stops I was funneled into a small clearing or amphitheater, completely hemmed in by greenbriar. Thinking there was no way out but to retrace my steps, I sat down behind a lichened rock to escape the wind and gather my wits. A hermit thrush appeared, and another secretive bird, the winter wren—my first for Soldiers Delight.

In summer this wren retreats to the mountains and the cooler North. Though its breeding in western Maryland was suspected for over a century, only in 1990 was the first nest with eggs found, among the sandstone outcrops and ledges near Oakland, in Garrett County. Come fall the winter wren slips east and south—in the colder months being commonest on Maryland's Eastern Shore—then departs again in spring for the land of hemlocks and rhododendrons.

The species is a shy "skulker" in the winter Piedmont, lurking beyond sight, *chipping* defiantly, skittering over logs like a dark vole, vanishing in cracks. It is impishly watchful in its frozen realm, bold for the briefest instant before it clams up and hides—hunkering down so doggedly thereafter that one wonders what it has to fear, what it husbands or guards in the stump-world, the cranny kingdom of wet-rot and hollow, moss-felted windfalls.

This particular wren carried out its usual mouselike maneuvers, eyed me briefly, barked its little double-chip call, and disappeared through the tangles. Soon rested and relaxed, and made to feel a part of things by the thrush and the wren, I spotted a niche in the undergrowth where the wren had disappeared. It turned out to be the head of a deer trail, which, by careful ducking under thorny bowers, I was able to follow to a stream. This shallow, half-frozen watercourse then became my footpath east, where I came out at one of the spots I had first been forced to retreat from. My toes were numb, and the wind in the clearing bit my cheeks, but I reveled in my clever persistence, and the memory of the thrush and wren.

January 25

Another cold, sunny day. I walked the eastern sector this morning, poking around in the serpentine prairies and grove edges. The lichens here are striking. Some adorn rocks, others tree roots and trunks, while many thrive on the ground in sunny glades, among the dormant grasses. Gray green reindeer lichen (*Cladonia* species) is a widespread genus, named as much for its prevalence in arctic tundras—where it is browsed by caribou, or "reindeer"—as for its antlerlike branches. It appears here in ground patches through much of the barrens. Lichens of the genus *Parmelia*, sometimes called boulder lichens, are another gray green group, with earlike edges. They are especially common in the oak and pine groves, where I noticed them speckling the oak trunks to a height of forty feet. I found red crest lichen, or British soldiers *(Cladonia cristatella)*, and pyxie cups *(Cladonia pyxidata)* to be common on rocks, soil, and fallen trees in both glades and groves. Over one hundred species of lichens have been identified at Soldiers Delight, including thirty-seven forms or varieties of the genus *Cladonia,* and thirteen of *Parmelia.*

Lichens are not as simple as they appear. They are actually two plants: a fungus and an alga living as one. The alga exists inconspicuously in the nets of threadlike mycelium below the more showy fungal layers. The relationship is symbiotic, that is, mutually beneficial. Unable to make chlorophyll for food, lichen fungi rely on their algae for carbohydrate production, while the algae benefit in turn from moisture and minerals gleaned by the fungi.

Reproduction is even more delicately balanced, and is usually achieved when parts of the plant are disturbed or break away. The lichen fungi produce spores that scatter, but the spores must scatter along with compatible algae, or new lichens can't form.

It was lichens that first helped create the serpentine soil. While clinging to rocks they secrete acids, and the loosened rock particles then lodge in cracks together with lichens that have died. This matter supports mosses and other higher plants that break the rock down further and slowly produce a soil—in the case of Soldiers Delight, a dry, minerally soil that supports few competitors.

January 28

Mild. It threatened rain, but I hiked up into the glades of the middle sector, above Ward's Chapel Road.

The prairies of Soldiers Delight are disappearing, and the main culprit is Virginia pine. What look like stable "pine barrens" to some visitors are in reality a recent phenomenon—in most places only seventy or eighty years old—that threatens to engulf the grasslands.

Virginia pine, sometimes called scrub pine, is a hardy species relatively resistent to serpentine minerals. Taking hold gradually among the outcrops as scattered and stunted trees, their roots break the rock, their debris mulches and shades the soil, and soon small groves come together. The groves shelter greenbriar and other herbaceous plants, until finally the soil structure is changed and supportive of rampant aliens.

If you dig down with a hard stick, as I did today, through the ground litter in one of these pine groves, you will quickly find fractured serpentinite like that out in the glades—the same stony "foundation," in fact, that nurtured unique floral associations just a few decades before but is now the floor of a forest. Without the fires once set by Native Americans, or the grazing of wild and domestic herbivores, the grasslands are becoming woodlands.

Soldiers Delight is fighting back. To the northeast I found several serpentine ridges that, with the help of ecologists and volunteers, have been cleared of pines and cedars and are littered only with their stumps.

January 31

Fine cold weather. I went to the park's western edge this morning to discover if any waterfowl are visible on Liberty Lake. Trudging uphill and down in the thick woods, I finally set up my tripod and spotting scope on the line between two

Soldiers Delight boundary trees (marked by yellow blazes), yet thanks to the bare branches I could make out a cove and section of deep water. I stamped my feet in the chill and kept peering through the lens. Twenty minutes later a pair of hooded mergansers swam around the bend. A quarter-hour past that, against the opposite shore, I made out the telling whiteness of a male common merganser.

The common and hooded mergansers are two of the most strange and beautiful water birds in North America. In the former species it is the female, not the male, who exhibits the striking head crest for which mergansers are noted, but the male's glossy deep green head and contrasting patterns of cream white and black upon chest, flanks, and wings are unusually handsome.

Meanwhile, the black and white semaphore crest of the male hooded merganser is so dramatic and surprising that its close-up viewing through lenses leaves some novice birders doubting what they have seen. The elegant bearing of the birds, who fold and unfold these crests in cryptic communication with their kind, is surpassed in grace only by their nimble diving, which occurs at frequent intervals as they glide amid coves and bays. Upon surfacing, they may shower the air with silver drops in an agile flexing of neck, head, and crest.

Yet what one actually sees of these two species is but half of their beautiful strangeness. They are agile and swift underwater, where they spend their secret hunting lives in pursuit of small fishes, literally flying beneath the surface. One need only throw stones in a stream, then view the panicked flash of minnows and bream, to imagine the speed of mergansers in being able to overtake them. And to savor their hydrodynamics, thrust your arm through deep water and gauge the force of resistance in this dense and dark liquid realm.

To compound their lovely oddity, these birds of the North do not nest on or beside the water they have mastered, but in hollow forest trees, usually so far from the shoreline that the young must be carried to it when ready to leave the nest.

February A Dual Preservation

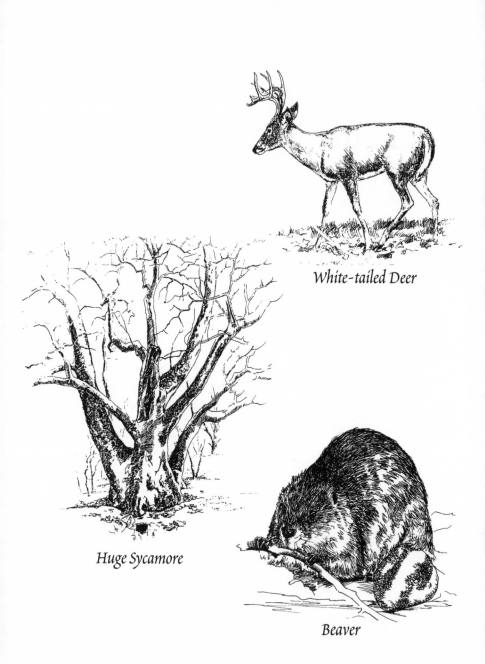

White-tailed Deer

Huge Sycamore

Beaver

February 4

Sometimes when I go off-trail, as I did this afternoon, in an obscure section of Soldiers Delight, I feel a vague sense of unease. It is the age-old apprehension about who or what might be lurking there, an anxiety about dangers so nameless that their very vagueness is worrying. Of course, this is furthered by the quite real knowledge that an injury or illness might leave me helpless in a place few know of or visit, and by the tales of murder and mayhem in the daily Baltimore papers.

But the feeling lasts only briefly. Invariably, if I proceed slowly and alertly, a kind of thrall overtakes me, and I move toward the other extreme. I arrive at a conviction of control—not control of the environment, but of my serene relationship with it, of my wish to take up its cup of beauty and drink it down, till I glow with wonder and excitement like one inspired by liquor. I am soon not merely carrying out an objective, as I viewed it at the start, but having a great time— the best time in days or weeks—making small discoveries right and left, above and underfoot, and enjoying, not enduring, my spooky drifting and aloneness.

I cannot name all that pleased me today. The *neet-neet* calls of unseen red-breasted nuthatches, the glimpse of a big red-tailed hawk rising off the forest and slanting across the clouds, the low sun piercing the branches and washing dark trunks with pale bars, and, when dusk approached, the city-bound gulls—mostly ring-billeds—flapping slowly like big lazy bats from out of the pink western sky. . . . these were but a few of the small glories that assailed me.

February 6

Deer Park Road follows a ridge that is a watershed "divide" of sorts. Generally, streams west of Deer Park flow to the Patapsco River (its north branch, dammed in 1953, being mainly Liberty Lake), and those to its east flow to Gwynns Falls, both waterways dumping into the Patapsco's "Middle Branch" at Baltimore Harbor, some fifteen miles southeast. Locust Run, one of the major arteries to the west, flows under Ward's Chapel Road near the southern border of Soldiers Delight, forming, as it enters Liberty Lake, a lovely cove favored by beaver. I found two lodges this morning, mounded collections of branches, on opposite banks. At this latitude, the winters being mild, the structures are not impressive and do not stand out.

More striking are the trees beaver have felled to build them, and to strip for food. One whole hillside on the north bank has lost a quarter of its timber, the stumps neatly gnawed to a point, like stockade posts, and littered round with wood chips. Yet, unlike men, the beaver don't seem to clear-cut, but move on when the slope is thinned. The freshest cuttings were south of the cove, on a sloping point.

This is technically City of Baltimore land; the lake is one of their water supplies (the Soldiers Delight boundary is further up on the hillside). Regardless, it's a beauty spot. Schistic shelves and boulders sit down in the jade-tinted water, the ridges glisten with mountain laurel or whisper with swaying pines, the hardwoods rise clean and stately. I have determined to come back often this month and clean up litter from the shore. I hauled out as much as I could today, in a bag I carry in my pocket.

February 9

After lunch, my wife, Donna, and I carried out a huge plastic bag full of cans and bottles, collected from the shoreline of the cove. Or part of the shoreline, anyway. As we sat on the point before heading back, the sun came out. A warm breeze rose, cutting the water and shaking the pines across the bay. We held hands like new lovers and listened to the wind song in the branches just above.

The affecting thing about soft, pine-bough wind song is that it is nothing much in itself. Like most whispers, it is audible only amid quiet, and thus heralds the retreat of clamor. It announces that all else is hushed, and that therefore murmurs may reign, the blown breath may be music, and the formless, the insubstantial, the next-to-nothing may triumph.

February 12

Sunny and cold. I spent most of the afternoon walking the northwest sector. A pileated woodpecker has chiseled out the side of an oak tree, in the woods above a stream. This buff yellow excavation is visible from afar and has left a midden of chips on the ground that is over three inches deep.

The hike back was special, for, in a manner I've noticed before, my fatigue played tricks with my mind, and as daylight died in the fields and the air thickened with a loamy vernal warmth, I was touched by some memory of childhood— some walk or car ride at dusk amid similar atmospherics. Below me and to the left a huge American sycamore (*Platanus occidentalis*) loomed, its pale dappled limbs, like those in my grammar school playground, enhancing my déjà vu. I walked down to this tree, at the low corner of a just-plowed field. Though not unusually tall, it is massive at its base, and sits at the mouth of a spring. No doubt this accounts for its size, being thus drought-proof throughout its life. The stone remnants of a springhouse form a gray horseshoe nearby. My sense of homage was immediate, and I sat down above the spring, my back against the trunk. I drank from my thermos here, the light went gold in the branches overhead and in a thicket above the field, and memories mixed and mingled. For two or three moments here and there, I was again ten years old. Thus do such walks become time machines, and the bases of trees their cockpits. At these places I will make regular rest stops on my marches and explorations.

February 15

Cloudy and spitting flurries. The sky in the northwest sector was the color of old pewter, and the air was damp and raw. It is the season of relative silence. In the sheltered woodland valleys, the great quiet of winter seems heightened by the prominence of otherwise trivial sounds: squealings of titmice and chickadees, leapings of squirrels through leaves, creakings of branch on branch.

It is also the season of easy access to all parts of the forest. With vines and ivy died back, a hiker has the run of slopes and hollows that in summer are choked or disguised. This morning I climbed uphill and down in the northern half of this sector, checking out ridges and ravines and enjoying the views through bare trees.

I wish we would get more snow. Tracks add spice to the

winter woods and prove the presence of animals that are otherwise hard to detect. Only in mud and by streams did I find any tracks today, and all of the commoner species: the handlike paw prints of raccoons on the very edges of the water, the hoof prints of deer in every spongy location, and a brief burst of red fox tracks, set down in a nearly straight line—the so-called "perfect walker" straightness of wild canines—on a sandbar at midstream.

February 18

Springlike weather. I took two bags over to the cove today, and filled the first one quickly. An old man hailed me from the trail, thinking I was fishing. He walked out to the point and began fishing himself, from a big boulder. I worked my way toward him along the shore, filling my second bag, then started a conversation when I reached him.

His name is Andy. He's lived here forty years, and remembers when there was no lake, and a fabric mill stood just to the west, where now there is only water. I pumped him about local wildlife. He said a black bear came through just five years ago. It was all of three hundred pounds, he knows, because his neighbor shot it in the backyard. The Department of Natural Resources got wind of this, came by to weigh and photograph it, and slapped the man's wrist for the violation. Andy also told me he himself raised Canada geese and wild turkeys, and let them go in the park. I disguised my disapproval.

Andy is nearly seventy and has heart problems. He did not fish long. I collected around the point and walked back with him. He was frequently breathless, especially on the last hill, when he stopped often. My own load was so heavy I didn't mind the stops. Andy gave me a smile and wave as he drove off in his pickup.

February 19

I called the DNR to confirm the black bear visit. I'm working up a mammal list, too, and take nothing for granted, especially local lore about creatures that are rare. A DNR policeman corroborated the story but could not provide a date. Black bears do wander, especially young males, from the western part of the state. I suppose I can count it. Sightings are one thing, a *corpus delicti* another.

The chief large mammal here is the white-tailed deer. They are present in nuisance numbers, overbrowsing the woods, getting into people's yards and gardens, eating up farm crops, and presenting a hazard to motorists. Various plans to thin them, through a special hunting season, have not met much success. Another problem they bring is the deer tick (*Ixodes dammini*). Much smaller than the wood tick (*Dermacentor andersoni*)—about the size of a pinhead—deer ticks are hard to detect on the body, but transmit a rare bacterium that causes serious illness. I have picked a few such ticks from my clothing in the last several seasons.

I see deer at Soldiers Delight on almost every outing. It is hardly worth noting, so regular is the event. Often it's just a fleeting glimpse—there is a snort and rustle of brush to alert me, then far off through the trees or tangles the huge white tails bob up, like someone shaking out bleached cotton dust mops, and the animals bound away with, well, the grace of deer. Common or not, I never tire of seeing them. The does and yearlings move together in small herds—up to twenty or thirty animals—and they'll come across a clearing single file, but spread way out, as if taking turns to impress me, with their wonderful shy head-turns and ear-cocks. Then the last one bounds and lands and finally bounds away, jerking its fluff-tail behind it toward the shadows, like a miffed child exiting a room with its bunny in furious tow.

February 21

I mentioned the big sycamore to Fraser today, and he knows of it. He thinks it may be a species state record, for the base is unusually broad at the point where such trees are measured. I will bring a tape there some time.

I also talked to him about cleaning up some of the junk near the tree and old springhouse. There are bottles, cans, tires—the usual assortment—on the ground, and an old oil drum in the creek below the spring. The oil drum got Fraser's attention, for the stream flows down to Liberty Lake in something less than a mile. He may get some of his summer "scouts"—local teens in a special program—to do some of the work.

Too much of Soldiers Delight's recent history is as a dump site. Until it became an official Natural Environment Area, nearby residents saw it as a wasteland where bulky items could be junked on the sly. Lacking good alternatives, even local farmers, some of whose land is now part of the N.E.A., would dump their broken machinery in a corner of the woods by their fields. Such corners became their private junkyards, forming a hard-trash record of their recent working lives. Today, Fraser still needs to block trailheads with boulders and big stumps, to keep folks from backing their loaded pickups in at night.

February 23

Springlike weather again. Donna and I parked by the overlook and walked southwest toward Red Dog Lodge. This stone cabin, built by a prominent local resident, Frederick Dolfield, in 1912, once lodged hunters in quest of rabbits and quail. Deer had been hunted out by the turn of the century, and were hardly more than a dream to those bivouacked at Red Dog Lodge. Their great numbers today would amaze the woodsmen of Dolfield's time. The lodge is locked against vandals now, but still functional, and is opened on special occasions. Its porch commands a fine view of the Carroll County hills to the west.

But a new building is upstaging Red Dog Lodge. We passed it on the way: a modern Visitor Center, under construction just to the east, at a cost of nearly one million dollars. It's the end result of decades of work by volunteers and planners. Without their efforts the N.E.A. itself, much less the new Center, would never have come into being.

Local residents were the first to take an interest in preserving this unique natural system. In 1959 the Citizens' Committee for Soldiers Delight was formed, and this group fought to have the area included in Maryland's State Master Plan. Then, in 1965, Soldiers Delight Conservation, Inc., was organized to raise funds for buying the property and making it a park. In four years they raised $25,000 from private donations. This was presented to the state, which, in 1970, began to acquire the land that now totals two thousand acres. Continued lobbying by determined individuals both within and outside government resulted in the state's final commitment to build a facility whose primary function would be environmental education.

We viewed the new construction, walked down to Red Dog Lodge, then out to some glades further west.

People are fond of dreaming about lost times and places. Many wish they could see things as they *really* were, once upon a time. Well, nowadays, in certain parts of Soldiers Delight, one can still see the distant past. For, in terms of the natural landscape, nothing much has changed.

We sat in such a place today. An open glade on a hillside gave us views to the north and west where no human structures showed. The dormant prairie fragment around us, ringed by thin oak groves and scattered pines, full of worn rock and pale grasses, was little altered from the past. A faint wind tickled the brown leaves under warm gray skies, just as it must have long ago. Blue jays delivered their ancient screech somewhere down by the stream, dark crows flapped overhead, and odors mixed in the false-spring air—warm earth scents ripe with vernal promise—just as they did for some farmer, some soldier, some nomad, in winters now centuries old.

Wild nature herself is a time machine. The fox or deer looks the same now as ever it did to our forebears. A tuft of grass or sedge predates the time of man in each unchanged detail. Of how many things in the modern world can this be truly said? Man may change the landscape, and even its list of inhabitants, but the inhabitants themselves—those that still survive—remain utterly unaltered.

Thus in places like Soldiers Delight there is a subtle dual

preservation at work. The changeless details of wild things come together in unchanged places—however small or fragmented—to give us glimpses of an ancient world largely thought to be long departed.

February 27

This morning, under a discarded truck tire at one of the farm-field junkyards, I found two big red-backed salamanders (*Plethodon cinerus cinerus*), each over four inches long. These are beautiful sleek creatures, shiny as oiled vinyl, with variable markings and colors. This pair showed the two most common appointments: the first had the lovely garnet-copper back that has given the species its name, and the second was a "lead-backed phase," that is, slate purple, shading almost into black, and this flecked lightly with gray. Their torsos are wonderfully lithe and supple, with small bent limbs fore and aft and finely delineated fingers. The bellies of each were pale pewter with salt-and-pepper sprinkles, and the way they were curled together in the mud made me think them a mated pair.

Salamanders show up in myth and folk legend, and were thought to have magical powers. All the elements are there. The most secretive of woodland creatures, they virtually disappear in full summer and winter, yet prowl about near the equinox, especially on misty nights. Their glistening, gem-toned bodies at times seem faintly translucent, and their elegant, often gaudy, markings must have offered a rare eyeful in the days before synthetic and aniline dyes. Fond of hiding under refuse near human habitation, they may appear and disappear from precise locations with uncanny regularity. Last year, for instance, I found another mixed pair under a similar discarded tire. When I lifted the tire the next day, just the red-backed was there. The day after that, there was only the lead-backed, and the fourth day there was neither, just a fat garden slug (Subclass Pulmonata) in the very spot they had rested. It's a bit like the old shell game: now you see them, now you don't, and who knows what will take their places. Quite often they reside under heavy rocks—seventy and eighty pounders that I need both hands to lift—yet are so delicately featured that the slightest rough handling may hurt them. How does such a fragile creature, ephemeral as the seasons, live compressed under massive stones, to enter and exit freely? Is there not some magic in that?

March *Unimproved by Science Fiction*

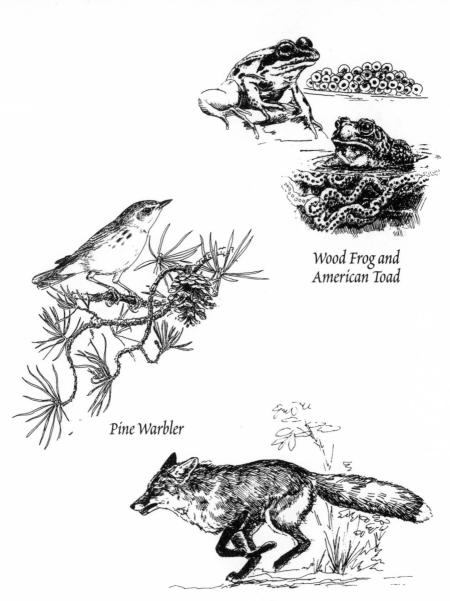

Wood Frog and
American Toad

Pine Warbler

Red Fox

March 1

There is something in approaching spring that draws me toward the clean and ordered. Perhaps the process of renewal is also a process of cleansing. In afternoon I did a final cleanup of the Locust Run cove, filling two more trash bags. When nearly finished, I observed through the gloom on a hillside some strange whiteness coating a fallen tree trunk. I feared, as I approached it, that someone had scattered cement or papier-mâché from a bucket, so much did the texture resemble these. Close up I concluded it was a fungus—the milk-white toothed polypore (*Irpex lacteus*), according to my field guide—covering several yards of the bark.

As I sat to drink my coffee an unpleasant musky odor alerted me to a large scrap of beaver fur that I was virtually on top of. The beaver had died and been consumed nearby, I decided, perhaps on this very spot, where the gnawed stump of a maple was serving as my backrest. I guessed it had been a young beaver, neither strong nor experienced, who let a big red fox surprise it as it worked on the tree at night.

I found the usual oddball assortment of junk along the shore, including a crossbow arrow, a homemade minnow net, and several rusted but unopened cans of beer, one of which sprayed me with fragrant brew when I popped it to empty the contents. I brought away three different fishing lures, hooks rusted away, including an Arbogast Jitterbug that I will fit with new hardware.

March 3

I went birding in the northwest sector with Dave Walbeck and Fraser Bishop. There were more hooded and common mergansers in the lake coves, and many fat fox sparrows. The fox sparrows are migrating now, and as I watched these it occurred to me that they are named not for the red fox, but the gray fox, for they share the gray's peculiar mottlings of both rust and pewter. Wood frogs (*Rana sylvatica*) were croaking by a stream, sounding from a distance like mallards. Dave turned over a log by the lake and bared a lovely red-backed salamander, as near in hue to metallic copper as I've seen. The morning warmed up nicely after a chilly start. At the cove, while showing them both an animal den I've discovered, which is tunneled between two rocks, a beaver surprised us by swimming past, quite unafraid, at an angle across the bay.

March 7

The preeminent legend of Soldiers Delight is that of the Berry's Hill hanging. In 1752, John D. Berry, a disgruntled twenty-year-old farmer, persuaded two indentured servant women to murder his stepparents in exchange for their freedom. Whether young Berry's own motive was hatred or property inheritance, or both, was never clearly learned, but the stepfather survived the servants' double knifing, and the three guilty parties were tried and convicted soon after at Joppa, the county seat. The sentence called for Berry, as instigator, to be hung from the highest point near the scene of the crime, and there to be suspended in chains from a crossbeam till his body rotted to the ground.

Aside from the mystery of motive (Berry professed his innocence to the end), the lingering controversy ever since has concerned the site of the hanging. Many still believe "Berry's Hill" corresponds to the present overlook off Deer Park Road. Others think it is just southwest of there, on an eminence where Red Dog Lodge now looks away to the west. Since the scene of the murder was a farm near the old village of Delight, several miles northeast of these sites, still others believe that the highest point "near the scene of the crime" could have been any of several hills in that direction.

Berry's Hill—"the Hanging Hill"—is in fact, I believe, a few hundred yards northwest of the Deer Park overlook, on a knob that the USGS cites as—at over 720 feet—the highest point in Baltimore County. A prominent regional landmark, and less than two crow-fly miles from the crime-site farm (whose location I determined from other evidence), it was well known in Berry's time, providing a fabled view that allowed one (in the days when most hills were clear-cut) to see the Blue Ridge to the west and the Chesapeake Bay to the east. These days, as I found out this morning, the hill is marked by two small geodesic survey slabs, a short distance west of Deer Park Road.

March 10

Clear and cold. Sally and Giles visited from Pennsylvania, with their two young boys, Evan and Eric. We all took a late morning walk together, at the Locust Run cove, and I showed them one of the beaver lodges. No beaver were about, but I presented Evan with a short wand of tree branch that a beaver had gnawed and barked. On the walk back I found a mass of wood frog eggs afloat in the puddled road. I scooped a few into a film canister, to see if they will hatch at home. Evan carried his beaver branch like a talisman.

The shy susceptibility that children bring with them—the fresh slate of their openness, well disguised by awkward movements and fumbling pronouncements—is deceptively broad and keen, receiving the pastels of nature in fullest array, aligning new sensations with primitive grandeur, producing portraits in a few deft strokes. The resulting naive image is so vividly composed that it often lasts them a lifetime. The rimed shoreline, the gnawed branch, the imagined keeper of the stick-lodge—all may be thin daily chaff to adults, but to children are the kernels of myth.

March 12

The skunk cabbage (*Symplocarpus foetidus*) are unfolding their little Turkish domes beside the creeks. Their flowers, which appear before the leaves, consist of the cowl-like spathe—which in profile often has the aspect of a tiny hunched-over penguin—and the hard ball of the spadix, covered with pentagonal scales, and which the "penguin" of the spathe, to pursue the metaphor, has enfolded at its base, as if sheltering an egg.

This common floodplain species is named for the skunky odor given off when its leaves are crushed. The young plants are edible if well dried and cooked, bringing a cabbage-greens quality to stews or soups, while the thoroughly dried roots can be ground to a cocoa-like flour.

March 14

In late afternoon I walked up into the far northeast corner of the eastern sector, which is mostly hilly farm fields and wooded edges.

Far across the plowed fields, along the top of a ridge, an adult red fox was running at full speed, occasionally turning its head to look back. Two hundred yards behind were a pair of large mixed-breed dogs, galloping in pursuit. It was not really a contest; the fox soon made the safety of the forest edge, and the dogs veered off over the hill at an easy lope. At that point a second fox sprang from the brushy edge below the slope, where the dogs had just passed, and moved in the direction of the first, though with complete casualness, aware that the chase was over. Such coddled farm dogs stand little chance of success in these encounters, and seem aware of it. Their pursuit was brief, exuberant, and blandly broken off, the way a puppy gives up his quest of a rabbit or butterfly across a well-trimmed lawn.

March 15

The skies cleared from yesterday's clouds and light rain. I went back to the same area and enjoyed a peaceful exploration among streams, woods, and fields. The sun got bright and the sky brilliant blue, and the leafless open-floored woodlands were full of almost as much light as they get in any season. This is what stirs the early wildflowers.

I discovered an unusually large and brilliant red-backed salamander under a log, the color being close to a maroon or oxblood of translucent luster. This was along a branch of Red Run, virtually under the canopy of a huge oak that rivals the big sycamore but is more compact. Unfortunately, if I remember it correctly from last summer, the tree is quite dead. It leans over a pool at a bend in the stream. Even dead it has a presence, and of course I drank my coffee beneath it, sitting on a ledge of tree roots and gazing down at some minnows moving suspended through the watery light and shadow. The air was sharp and slightly musty, the base of the woods beyond was dappled with amber sunshine. Angling up and away from my right shoulder was the main trunk, tilted just above horizontal at first, carpeted on its topside with green moss, then thrusting skyward at a steeper angle, the whole of it like some ascending pathway to the heavens. I sat some minutes in a trance, the water gurgled above the pool, and a lone tufted titmouse called faintly from afar, *peter-peter-peter* ... *peter, peter, peter,* with what seemed unnatural persistence.

March 17

This morning Donna and I walked the northwest sector. As we left the parking area west of Ward's Chapel Road, I looked up to see an adult bald eagle soaring against the blue. It was probably in migration north. I have now seen both North American eagle species at Soldiers Delight, for I found an immature golden eagle, by far the rarer of the two, in the eastern sector the autumn before last. It had been perched high in a dead tree not a hundred feet away, and I inadvertently spooked it as I passed. Unlike the adult, which is uniformly dark with tawny highlights, the immature golden eagle has a white-banded tail and white wing patches, and these were apparent as it pushed aloft and circled in the autumn air.

Our spring bald eagle, meanwhile, displaying the pure white head and tail of the mature bird, did not linger but kept a northeasterly course, sailing higher in gigantic circles, till it was soon out of sight. Had I not looked up when I did, the brief spectacle, like so many events in nature, would have easily passed unnoticed.

March 20

A mild day. I went walking in a nearly pure stand of tulip-trees, or yellow poplar (*Liriodendron tulipifera*) in the northwest sector. Eastern phoebes were about, rasping their calls on the hillsides. There was another winter wren as well, who pinched himself between rotting logs in an effort to keep hidden, and an eastern bluebird in a pasture beyond the woods. I sipped coffee and ate a donut in the splendid empty groves. All others were away working and keeping busy, while I alone was left to appreciate this quiet oasis amid the vast tumult of cities and suburbs. The things I imagine here, the sensations I feel when alone in these "dead spots" of civilization, are untranslatable. They make most problems bearable.

Today I did not want to leave the woods, and was especially calm and relaxed, and took my time about everything.

There is a leisureliness in nature, an aspect of immeasurable slowness—especially among the plants—that breaks the rhythm of haste demanded by the world of men. Some contend that humans are descended from tiny mammals—shrewlike creatures of wild energy and hunger. When I see people in our urban hives I have little reason to doubt it. Thus I seek out lazy forests at all times of the year. The late winter groves seem particularly at peace. Though each tree fights for survival with others, it proceeds at a pace beyond our immediate grasp, thus preserving the illusion of passivity. Such illusions seem best in these umber leave-strewn dells, washed by broken shadows, settled with the reek of wood rot, guarded by columnar boles. They comfort when nothing else can. The tree—that thing so utterly alien from the muscle and blood realm of apes—is thus an alien to be cherished, an alien unimproved on by any science fiction.

March 21

One of the wood frog eggs hatched today. The tiny tadpole, like a black peppercorn with a tail, thrashed about in its jar on the sill when confronted with movement or sunlight.

How different is this jar-world from the tadpole's home in the muddy road rut, where, threatened by drought or vehicle, malicious hiker or hungry beast, it must metamorphose quickly, and escape if it can on new-formed limbs, to the relative safety of the woods. Here, in the jar, it has cushions of time and space, and need not hurry its growth. Of course, quite oblivious to luxury, it lives on the razor's edge, has evolved amid imminent disaster, been forged by peril and urgency. It proceeds with identical speed through its various transformations, regardless of nearby conditions.

Relative to the tadpole, modern Americans have numerous options, broad margins of safety, and need not program their growth along blind, inflexible lines. Yet at times are they not like the tadpole? insistent on rigid growth or progress in one direction, refusing to slacken pace, rejecting a change of course, proceeding as if on the razor's edge though cushioned at every margin.

March 24

I tramped the eastern sector this morning, paying special attention to the prairie glades and pine groves. A rich, persistent trilling I at first took for the spring song of the northern junco before realizing it was a pine warbler. In the next hour I heard or saw at least seven. This is the earliest warbler to return here, and I believe they've been around for several days already, so their arrival more or less coincides with the equinox. It is even possible that one or two overwinter.

When birds first appear on breeding territory from the south, they are highly vocal. These pine warblers were no exception. The greenish yellow males mounted swaying branches of Virginia pine and pitched their loose trill into the March wind, then flashed back next to the dark trunk as shyness overtook them. In this manner they moved from tree to tree within what was to be their turf, and where boundaries came together there were fierce duels of song. Yet the progress of spring is slow and incremental. But for this one species, the pine groves were silent. Sun heated the serpentine between wet depressions, tufts of last year's grasses shivered in the wind, and pitch scent wafted with the warbler song, through lanes in the stunted groves.

March 26

Once again I am drawn to the watery places of Soldiers Delight. In the morning I followed a stream in the northwest sector called Pines Branch, from the spot where it enters Liberty Lake, upstream until it disappears beneath the sloping farm fields. The skunk cabbage domes line the banks in great abundance now, and I take some care not to crush them underfoot. There is no sight or sound of the waterthrushes yet, which surprises me only slightly.

I rested on a large fallen tree trunk that almost spans the creek near an elbow bend. I could not determine its species. It is really just a rotted log at present, richly rugged with moss that was chartreuse in the sunlight, dull jade in the shade. The water purled and gurgled at two locations, behind and before me, where the flow was blocked by sand and debris but had found some narrow breach. I sat cross-legged and looked down into a pool perhaps eighteen inches deep.

Many water striders (*Gerris marginatus*) were skating the surface, and the raised welts of surface film, where their legs met the water, threw dark ovals of shadow on the sandy bottom. A single strider throws six of these welt shadows below, one for each leg. The complete formation—a pair of ovals in front, a pair behind, and a smaller one to each side—rather resembles the paw print of some mammal. As the striders skate above, the shadow ovals mimic every movement at refracted angles below. What I discovered today is that a mating pair—and there were several on the water—throws not twelve oval shadows, or even six, but eight. Only two flanking leg shadows of the top-mounted male appear below, added to the six of the female. The alignments reminded me not only of paw prints, but of horses in harness. The "four horses" of the "coach-and-four" single, with its two outrider dots, become a "coach-and-six" during mating: six oval shadows, aligned in three pairs like a stagecoach team, are projected on the bottom, and the side dots make eight.

March 27

I couldn't resist returning to Pines Branch today, and was rewarded on my way by the sight of a large wild turkey, a tom, crossing the plowed fields just above there. When he saw me he ran quickly to the woods, with a comical rolling gate, jarring side to side with each stride like an unbalanced load, which indeed this fat one was.

The thrill was tempered by my thoughts of Andy the fisherman, who not only raised and released such birds, as I remembered him telling me, but trained them to respond to his calls, to afford him a kind of "gobbler rapport" while hiking. This selfish and perverse wildlife tampering, besides reflecting the worse kind of Walt Disney animal-buddy sentimentality, threatens the truly wild populations with the introduction of barnyard diseases. And, of course, it ruins the pleasure of wild discovery for hundreds of people like myself.

The wild turkey, of which there are six geographic subspecies, was once so abundant in North America that it was a candidate for our national emblem. By 1900, loss of habitat and intense hunting pressure had reduced its numbers to near zero in many regions, including the East. Reintroduction and reforestation have brought it back, though the former practice is not one for amateurs.

I ended up with thirty-two bird species for the morning, including a sharp-shinned hawk. Sharpies, which are strictly cold weather visitors in the area, will soon be moving north and west to breed, to the relief of the many small birds on which they prey. I also found three more red-backed salamanders, and the largest eastern hemlock (*Tsuga canadensis*)—perhaps sixty feet tall—that I've seen here to date, which of course became yet another of my rest stop trees.

March 31

Donna and I walked the southern half of the northwest sector this morning. A few skunk cabbage are still in flower, but most have assumed their bright green large-leafed habit, which offers a lovely accent along the brownish stream banks.

On our return we discovered, in a flooded road rut, a long

egg chain, or "necklace," of the American toad (*Bufo americanus*). One's first thought is of a bicycle chain discarded in the mud, for the jellylike links of the strand are so configured. This necklace also resembled somewhat an animal intestine, the fine silt of the puddle having obscured the black embryo dots that would have quickly shown the links to be eggs. Though the many twists and overlaps of the necklace made it difficult to judge, I estimated its length at over nine feet. Such a modest creature, the toad, to reproduce with such profligance.

April This Outcry of Joy

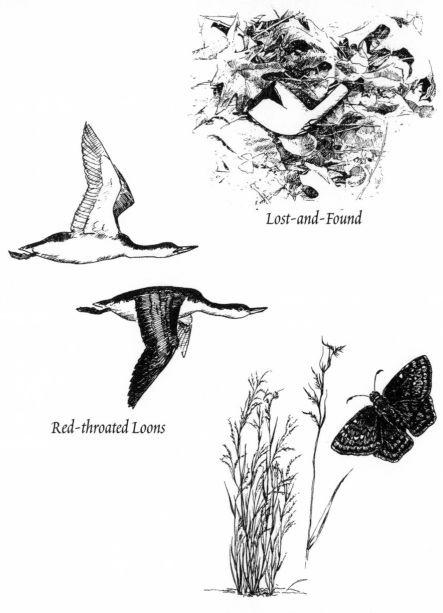

Lost-and-Found

Red-throated Loons

Bluestem and Dusky-Wing

April 3

That little psychic trap—the false vernal confidence of April, the fake promise of steady warmth—has arrived as it should, with days both sunny and mild.

While hiking a corner of the northwest sector, I discovered thousands of tiny springtails (*Achorutes nivicolus*) on the leaves at the base of an oak. These wingless, primitive insects feed on leaf mold and algae, and are common—though little noticed—in cool woodlands, often dotting the snow in winter.

On the tulip-trees I sometimes observe grayish white bands an inch or two thick, at various heights on the trunk. They look like man-made blazes, but are apparently some sort of ribbon-shaped mold or lichen.

Along a high trail I found some lovely round-lobed hepatica (*Hepatica americana*). What appear to be petals are actually sepals, and vary a lot in both number and color. The first plant I found had six "petals" of pure white, and the second, a few yards further along, had eight of lavender blue. I also found wood anemone (*Anemone quinquefolia*) on the ridge above the mill. Both species, of course, are not serpentine wildflowers, but those of richer, deciduous woods, of which the northwest sector is heavily composed.

The stream near Oakland Road, which has no name that I know of, lies just below the northern boundary of Soldiers Delight. An old water mill that was used for crushing quartz and is sometimes called the Ware Mill, still stands some hundred yards upstream from a cove of Liberty Lake. It now has a cement-block base, though remnants of a fieldstone foundation just behind it suggest more than one incarnation. The mill was most active in the 1880s, when local farmers brought quartz chunks from their fields to be ground here for use in abrasives.

An extensive outcrop of schist forms a low cliff above the south bank here. On it I found several lovely colonies of mosses and lichens, some literally attached to each other in their profusion. As I examined them I noticed a man and teenage boy land their Old Town canoe at the cove and walk toward the mill. Halfway there they spotted me, did an about-face, and double-timed back to their unguarded canoe. I am always alert for humans when afield, the only creatures that worry me. Partly out of distrust, and partly from the wish for solitude, I try to see or hear them first, then avoid them completely. I guess others share my perspective, and find *my* presence bothersome. Such attitudes are a comment on the times, and—in the case of this man and boy—on the cost of Old Town canoes.

April 5

I visited the eastern sector. There are still few migrant bird species about, so I contented myself with pine warblers as I crossed the glades, and with several eastern phoebes.

In the deciduous floodplain of the northeast corner, almost within the shadow of the big dead Red Run oak, I sat down on a midstream gravel bar. An odd shape caught my eye, and I picked up part of an old clay tobacco pipe. Nearly all of the bowl was intact, and an inch or two of the stem. The bowl was maybe an inch across, the stem straight and thin, and a maker's mark, which looked like the letter *G*, was stamped upon the side. There was a pretty leaflike emblem detailed in relief along the base. The pipe is certainly old, probably nineteenth century, maybe older. Recent rains have no doubt washed it out of the bankside where it was buried, for nothing so fragile would have survived long in the rocky stream itself. I wrapped it carefully in a small towel I carry in my pack, after first observing a moment of appreciative silence in the presence of the looming oak.

April 8

Perhaps there is something to this big tree business, to my superstitious notion that such old and gigantic forms enfold some auspicious aura. Today, while resting under the big sycamore in the northwest sector, I was tempted to upend a rusted iron tractor wheel that lay half-buried in the leaves. Under it were three red-backed salamanders and a pair of northern two-lined salamanders (*Eurycea bislineata bislineata*). This established my own record for salamanders under a single object (five), but also gave me my first two-lined species at Soldiers Delight. I usually find two-lined salamanders in or very near their favorite streams, but these were on high, dry ground, thirty feet from the water. Nor have I ever found red-backs and two-lineds together at the same spot. It was a happy little occasion of small, private anomalies.

Rationalists, and I'm proud to call myself one, might mock my enthusiasm for the sense of "fortuitous encounter" I feel when stationed beside these forest giants. They might say, with no need to mythologize them, that very large trees are already awesome phenomena, being ecological microsystems that nurture and protect whole worlds of related flora and fauna. The ancient "old growth" conifers of the Pacific Northwest are valued for just this complex vitality, as are the giants of the tropical rain forests, with their many unique epiphytes and canopy insects.

Thus my occasional witness to their larger influence on my puny human world—the kismet of daydreams, clay pipes, and wheel-dwelling salamanders—pales before this science, is mere random triviality. Which dampens my pleasure not a jot. I often worship at the throne of science but am also a bit of a heretic. There are chinks in my pragmatist's armor. I believe in the power of the trivial event to inspire ones much larger, and in the disproportionate influence of that rational flotsam we call whimsy. I make room for the unmeasurable, the ineffable, the intuitive. A subordinate belief in the nonrational is essential, I contend, if only as a jump-start to discovery. My "Jeep of Natural Exploration" is driven by a scientist, but he sometimes takes direction from a pagan seated in back.

April 9

I have received information from the Center for Urban Archeology in Baltimore. Very helpful people. From the photocopies they provided I've determined that my clay pipe is probably a "short clay" (an abbreviated, straight-stemmed clay pipe of the late nineteenth century), most likely the Scottish cutty (circa 1885), or something patterned after it, with a variation on the common oak-leaf emblem at its base.

It is probably difficult to be more precise than that without having it scrutinized by an expert. Short clays were favored by working men of the day and were produced by the thousands. They were so cheap in some areas that they were given away with a mug of beer by local saloon keepers, which ranks them in relative scarcity with our modern matchbooks.

Still, it is a nice little link with the forgotten past. The bowl has a delicate feel, is smooth and cool to the touch, and the raised emblem at the base is finely wrought. Perhaps it was a common item, but it in no way resembles the mass produced products of today, with their lack of subtlety and character. And to know that I was the first human being to touch it again after over one hundred years provokes a quiet thrill. It will make a good item for the new Soldiers Delight Visitor Center, which is scheduled for completion this summer.

April 10

I hiked up into the northwest sector. Spring is emerging slowly, the green leaves and buds still shy, though the pink pre-leaf flowers of eastern redbud (*Cercis canadensis*) offer accent here and there. A mammal den dug high into an embankment near a stream, and which I first noticed last winter, has been excavated further. The tunnel goes in under the roots of a big hardwood, and the tailings, which cascade down the embankment across some forty square feet, are entirely of sand. From the size of the entrance and the location, I suspect it belongs to a raccoon.

The Louisiana waterthrushes were at last apparent in the floodplains. They seemed stingy with their noted ethereal song but readily piped their alarm or "chip-note," as I reached the margins of the creeks. At one point, when I had walked a hundred yards of stream bank and been chipped at loudly by one bird, a second bird just ahead took up the scolding. Both sexes look alike, so whether these were two males defending successive territories, or the mated male and female of a single turf, I could not guess. As I left the floodplain one favored me with his song, a vigorous short warble that then sucks and strangles at the close, tapping ever so slightly the sweet sadness of echo and expiration.

April 12

Again I was up in the northwest. I've taken to calling the nameless stream there Mill Run, as the old quartz mill is a notable feature, and indeed the only such mill in Soldiers Delight.

Another, subtler feature runs beside Mill Run for about a quarter mile, but has been noted by virtually no one: not the USGS, nor even, to my slight surprise, the people who made Fraser Bishop's map. This is often the way with sunken roads. What appears to be merely a woodland path was at one time part of a thoroughfare. In the days before hard surface, roads were often of dirt or sand. This is no revelation. Yet few realize that in disuse such bare highways, before vegetation can stabilize them, become natural courses for runoff, and erosion slowly sinks them. Of course, they have stopped being repaired, so sections, especially along slopes, may drop five or six feet, leaving a flat narrow plain below a wall-like earthen ridge. The south "wall" here is over a yard high, utterly overgrown, and the old bed now sports several trees that rise twenty and thirty feet. But once one sees through the camouflage, it is unmistakably a road.

On the way back, I was reminded again how quickly trees

reclaim land. There is an old field near the middle of this sector, maybe ten acres in size. I followed the main trail through it and was struck by the height and density of saplings growing up amid grass and bramble. Red maple (*Acer rubrum*), black cherry (*Prunus serotina*), sassafras (*Sassafras albidum*), flowering dogwood (*Cornus florida*), and Virginia pine are the early, fast-growing colonists. Tulip-trees and assorted oaks and hickories are not far behind, and will shade out most of the others. An uncut field becomes a forest around here in only a few decades. A friend of mine recalls bobolinks and bobwhites from a meadow of his fifties childhood, where now there is deepest woods.

April 14

At the library I found an interesting early map of Baltimore County, dated 1850. At that time only one main road, Deer Park, traversed what is now Soldiers Delight. The principal residents east of Deer Park were the Pennys, the Fords, the Lockhards, the Churches, the Dunkins, the Lowes, and the Walters. To the west were the Allens, the Barrys, the Wares, the Gosnells, the Vaughns, and the Lowes again.

The main east-west thoroughfare, just south of Soldiers Delight, was Liberty Road, along the north side of which lived the Wards, Maddocks, Chapmans, and Worthingtons. A large grist and saw mill stood north of Liberty Road where it crosses the Patapsco. Lyons Mill Road also cut east and west below the present park boundaries, connecting both Liberty and Deer Park Roads and forming the distinctive little triangle that still exists today.

To the north, branching off Deer Park Road, was Delight

Road, which headed eastward toward the village of the same name, between Owings Mills and Reisterstown. Near Delight, at the intersection of the Delight Road and Cherry Lane, was the old Clark farm, where John Berry incited murder in 1752.

What is now Soldiers Delight, however, was for a long time just a fragment of the vast tract called Soldiers Delight Hundred. Mentioned in records as early as 1660, parts of what are now Anne Arundel, Baltimore, Howard, Carroll, and Frederick Counties once fell within its bounds. Around 1750 it began to be parceled systematically by local governments, until only the present barrens, known of old as the "White Grounds," (perhaps for the pale overall aspect of the rocky prairies) were still called Soldiers Delight.

April 16

Wildflowers now carpet the richer woodlands in profusion. Common blue violets (*Viola papilionacea*), spring-beauties (*Claytonia virginica*), and bluets (*Houstonia caerulea*) dot the still brownish ground with blues, pinks, and whites, and with the green of tender leaves. The single creamy blossom of bloodroot (*Sanguinaria canadensis*) has unfolded in places on the hillsides. A member of the poppy family, bloodroot thrusts its flower upward from a curled, deep-lobed leaf, the eight to ten petals being fully spread in sunlight, half-closed in dappled shade, and clenched shut at night. The stems and roots, if severed, exude a staining, orange red or brownish juice, which resembles drying blood. Bloodroot blooms but briefly in spring, in some spots for several weeks, in others for a matter of days.

I found a green-backed heron at the pond in the northwest

sector, and a pair of Louisiana waterthrushes were stalking the Mill Run banks, bobbing as they moved. One had a stronger yellowish patch below the wing than the other, and I couldn't help thinking this was the male, for the colors of male birds generally, are enhanced in spring. Yet the field guides insist "sexes alike" for waterthrushes.

Blue-gray gnatcatchers were about, wheezing and chattering faintly in the high and middle branches, and seeming to enjoy the sunlight. And a loud *wick-up!* from a clump of bushes steered me to my year's first Acadian flycatcher, the tiny greenish bird that, like the gnatcatcher, will breed through much of Soldiers Delight.

April 17

This morning, as I walked the southern end of the northwest sector at about ten o'clock, I spied an osprey rising just above the trees. Soon after there were three broad-winged hawks. Next a northern harrier was up, and finally a red-shouldered hawk. All but the latter are likely to be migrants, and since each was low when spotted, then soared up and away toward the north, I deduced they were catching the morning's first thermals, and, more importantly, that they all spent the night at Soldiers Delight.

I then remembered seeing two hawks come down in our woodlot at dusk the night before. Clearly, the day before was a big one for hawk migration, and it seems likely that Soldiers Delight is a favorite overnight roost. The idea that an April evening hiker, perhaps myself, might walk unaware below this many—or far more—raptors, and that each might look down on him undetected, was pleasant food for thought.

I next observed three red-throated loons, strung out at long intervals, winging steadily northward. In flight, with their slender necks outstretched, they look a bit like mergansers, but loons trail their big webbed feet out behind. The common loon has a larger head and feet, and slower wing beats, and is usually later in migration. Many birders don't know that, from just after dawn till midmorning, even far inland on still April days, both loon species may easily be seen if one pays some attention to the sky.

After this I was sensitized. Every bird seemed lovely, each wildflower special. I positively dawdled. On the walk back, as I started to emerge from the woods, a palm warbler perched by the trail and posed as I watched it in the sunlight. Beautiful bird! I actually shouted this aloud, though no one was in earshot. It's a common species in migration, but I hadn't seen one in a year, and it seemed the essence of color, grace, and springtime. The elation of a fine outing had expanded, as it sometimes does, like a bubble, and had burst in this outcry of joy.

Still kicking inside with contentment, I walked the edge of the farm fields toward my car. In the dirt of the trail was an object, a coin or plug of metal, and I stooped to extract it. A novelty item, from a carnival or convention, was my first thought. There were stars around the edge; the copper had gone green. But I soon saw it was an old U.S. coin, badly corroded, the date just legible: 1885.

Here was the icing on my already gilded day. The last quarter-mile I spent whistling.

April 18

I rose early to go fishing in the Locust Run cove of Liberty
Lake. It was just getting light when I got my canoe to the
bank, where I began fitting my gear. A loud tail-slap on the
water only ten yards out from shore was my introduction to
the beaver. The first was soon joined by a second, and they
continued slapping loudly till I got my canoe in the water.
Then a third chimed in, and the hubbub got that much
worse. I had never seen this many wild beaver at one time; it
was fascinating, but, as they no doubt intended, made my
mission all but impossible.

One beaver, perhaps a male, was quite fearless, charging the
canoe head-on, veering off a few yards from the bow, then
tucking and smacking with its tail as it dove. The abrupt tuck
motion of diving makes a hollow preliminary slurp or blurp,
followed by the slap, so the typical sound of beaver disapproval is a quick, two-part *klub-blam!* or *blub-blew!,* and a
crater of concentric wavelets then expands in all directions.

Your average fish finds this disconcerting, or so I reasoned.
I paddled beyond the cove, to the first little bay to the north.
Still one beaver followed. Along the shoreline, from one hundred yards away, he swam in a straight line toward me, then
turned nearby at a sharp angle and delivered a final smash. If
ever I saw an animal mark territory, it was this surveyor of a
beaver.

Perhaps I was too distracted, but I caught no fish, not even
with my recycled Jitterbug. It hardly mattered; there were
plenty of other distractions, which is why I like to fish. The
shadbush (*Amelanchier arborea*) was in bloom; its white
petals flecked the water. A black-and-white warbler squeaked

from a shoreside hardwood, a waterthrush sang from Pines Branch, and a great blue heron sailed over with casual grace, legs dangling loosely, wings flapping just hard enough to stay airborne, which seemed not very hard at all. Near the end I was treated to my second loon event in as many days, this one an extravaganza. For nearly a quarter-hour they came over, in ones, twos, and threes. I counted eighteen in all, red-throated loons in migration north, strung out against the overcast, arrow-necks into the wind, dipping their wings like oars.

April 21

I have consulted several books, and my corroded U.S. coin, about the size of a modern quarter, turns out to be a "large cent," the copper penny of its day. Because they stopped minting these about 1857, I closely reexamined the date, and found it to be not 1885, but 1835, a half-century earlier than I had thought. Almost four million large cents were minted in that year, and while in such condition it has little collecting value, it will make a fine artifact for display at the Visitor Center.

My wood frog tadpole now has limbs front and back, though its tail still hangs on. I shall release it soon.

April 23

Most of the grasses are still quite dormant in the eastern glades. I heard the first prairie warbler singing there this morning, and found a painted lady butterfly (*Vanessa cardui*) of miniature proportions, which is typical of the year's first brood.

So many natural events are unfolding now that it is difficult to concisely note them all. The drumming of red-bellied woodpeckers on hollow trees has become unusually loud and persistent. Both sexes do this but especially the males, to define territory and initiate mating. The field sparrows are also singing loudly, in competition with other males and, perhaps, with the prairie warblers, who share similar habitats and song qualities.

I saw my first dragonfly of spring, an eastern blue darner (*Aeshna verticalis*), above a rye field. A woodchuck near there disappeared into a den that has three entrance holes.

The wing-shaped key fruits or "samaras" of red maple were quite dense on one tree, and salmon pink in the sunlight. Bark is a poor indicator of species, as this tree showed, for it was blackish and furrowed at the base, stubbly gray further up, and quite pale and smooth near the top.

I found yet another sunken road, well grown up with saplings, and not on any of the maps. Its walls were lined with the crenulated leaves of gill-over-the-ground (*Glechoma hederacea*), bright green and rampant, and soon to bloom.

Ruby-crowned kinglets in migration are replacing the golden-crowned kinglets so numerous this winter, and bluets are alive in the barrens, where on my return I found a dark, early species of skipper known as juvenal's dusky-wing (*Erynnis juvenalis*).

Skippers are related to true butterflies, the differences being largely their thick, mothlike bodies and their hook-tipped antennae, which are spread wide at their bases and, at their ends, curved back toward the wings. There is a quality of "skipping" in their addled flight. Numerous, look-alike species make them hard to identify in the field, but their restricted range and seasonal appearance help to limit the possibilities.

The chief range-limiting factor among skippers, like that of most butterflies, is the fact that their larvae, or caterpillars, are "plant-specific": that is, they feed only on plants of a certain family or genus. There are, for instance, five species of skippers at Soldiers Delight whose larvae require grasses of the genus *Andropogon*. These are the well-known prairie grasses that dominate the glades here—the most prominent being little bluestem (*Andropogon scoparius*). Without the bluestems and their *Andropogon* relatives, this quintet of skipper species would vanish from Soldiers Delight, and indeed from any other place where such grasses were destroyed. Evolution has linked these invertebrates, as it has many others, not merely to plants, but to distinctive *types* of plants, without which they are doomed.

April 25

As I drove down Ward's Chapel this morning, I came upon a man directing traffic around an object in the road. I saw it was a black rat snake (*Elaphe obsoleta obsoleta*), so I pulled over and got out. The man explained in a nervous voice that the snake had fallen from a tree branch above the road, nearly hitting him as he walked along. He was afraid of snakes, he said, yet here he was directing cars away from one. The snake was reluctant to move, as a European starling was wedged halfway down its throat. I found a large stick and prodded it toward the shoulder, whereupon it disgorged the bird and, after several moments of halfhearted hissing, headed into a pasture. Even this man's fear of serpents was not enough to let him watch it be destroyed, which says something for the benign influence of wildness and nature.

In the northwest sector, both the white-eyed vireo and yellow-throated vireo were calling in their different habitats, and in their very different voices. The former sounds strident and wrenlike, playing peekaboo from tangled edges, while the latter is a hesitant, throaty caroler of the forests, more in tune with its family.

Several species of ferns were unfolding their fiddle heads, and parasitic brown-headed cowbirds were creaking and chirping as they searched the woods, hoping to locate other nests where they will lay their unwelcome eggs like that fabled deceiver, the cuckoo. They especially target warblers, whose already shaky reproduction is thus further threatened.

The white flowers of rue anemone (*Anemonella thalictroides*) bloomed widely on forest slopes, while the pink, half-clenched petals of slender toothwort (*Dentaria heterophylla*) I found but rarely.

Up on the highlands near the mill, amid the mountain laurel, there are large patches of club-mosses, those evergreen relatives of the ferns. I noted two species today: running ground pine (*Lycopodium complanatum*), with its erect, coniferlike branches only inches off the ground, and tree club-moss (*Lycopodium obscurum*) which has a compact outline and a prickly stem.

The club-mosses and ground pines comprise a group known as "fern allies," ancient plants—not mosses at all but closely related to horsetails (*Equisetum*)—that were once very large and dominated the landscape over two hundred million years ago. The ground pines carry reproductive spores on erect cylinders which resemble tiny pine cones. In club-mosses, a bulblike case at the base of their leaves holds the spores.

About one hundred club-moss species exist worldwide, and many have commercial uses. Unfortunately, the practice of combining them in Christmas wreaths has almost destroyed several species. While the spores of some tropical club-mosses were once used for coating pills to keep them from becoming sticky, still other spores, which flash briefly when ignited, were used in making fireworks.

Among butterflies, the first spicebush swallowtails (*Papilio troilus*) are about, as are the small dark sooty-wings (*Pholisora catullus*). As I left the woods a vast assemblage of crows, perhaps a hundred in all, were harassing a great horned owl, with calls and shrieks so violent that being nearby was unpleasant.

April 28

Another breeding wood warbler at Soldiers Delight, besides the pine and the prairie, is the blue-winged warbler. Today I heard one in the brushy pasture south of Mill Run, doing its familiar *beee-bzz*. A second song, sounding from a distance like a blue-winged variation, turned out to be that of the migrant black-throated blue warbler voicing an atypical song.

The songs of migrating warblers are confusing even to experts. It is not simply a matter of memorizing field guides or tapes, nor even of gaining experience to the point where you know them by heart. Of course, all of these techniques help. But no one truly knows the songs by heart, because no two birds are identical. Each is an individual, who had different parent teachers, responds to different rivals, differently, in different kinds of habitat, in different stages of maturity and health, at different latitudes on earth. One acquaints oneself with "typical" songs—models, as it were, of characteristic patterns in the voice of a given species. But there is always a margin of variance, and even with perfect recall each spring (*much* rarer than birders will admit), a birder must know that singing males, while bidden by physiology and the dictates of heredity, are affected by quirks and foibles like all the higher animals.

There are many lovely yellow violets (*Viola rotundifolia*) blooming along the wooded streams, and jack-in-the-pulpit (*Arisaema tryphyllum*) are rising.

I explored the rock-lined remnants of an old kiln or furnace, looking without success for snakes or salamanders. Just above it is the pit of the old Weir Mine, several hundred feet deep. At one time it was the largest chrome working in the county. Its remains are now well guarded by a fence.

April 30

On my return walk this morning, Fraser approached me in his pickup to say that I'd left my car lights on. A second man in the cab was a *Baltimore Sun* reporter, and we chatted after checking out my car. He's doing a story on the John Berry hanging and wants to know the location of the "Hanging Hill." I led them to the highest point in Baltimore County, just off Deer Park Road, where I think it was. I pointed out the geodesic markers, and also, by the way, the indigenous birdfoot violet (*Viola pedata*), a beautiful and uncommon species which yet made no impression on our visitor. Back at

Fraser's house we confirmed, from several of his maps, that this hill is indeed the high spot, at 724 feet.

The reporter was not convinced. The article he has in mind will promote the new Visitor Center, as well as the legend of the hanging, and he seemed intent on linking both. Despite having done a fair amount of research, he more than once made the comment, complete with broad smiles and excited gestures, that, by God, in the final story he was going to place that hanging smack in front of the Visitor Center, as if Fraser or I would consider such fabrication a welcome publicity perk.

It is no mere coincidence that the hills of Soldiers Delight are the highest in Baltimore County. The component ultra-mafic rocks and related minerals of serpentinite outcrops weather a bit more slowly than those around them, leaving them generally higher than the lands nearby. The names of other regional serpentine formations speak well of this: Bare Hills, Blue Mount, Chrome Hills, Serpentine Ridge. This height, combined with the exposed rock faces, little or no topsoil, a vertical network of cracks and fissures that quickly sheds water, and the high latent heat retention of imbedded rocks like soapstone (massive blocks of which, in other lands, were once quarried by the Vikings and placed beside their bonfires to throw heat through the long polar nights), make the serpentine slopes unusually dry and sunstruck.

Botanists use the term "xeric" to describe very dry habitats, and their adapted plants are called "xerophytes." Some of Soldiers Delight's xerophytes are now in bloom; others are just beginning to flower. Blossom-time comes early on the serpentine outcrops, which lie now like elevated griddles under the nearing flame of the vernal sun.

May *So Nicely Shut Apart from Man*

Whip-Poor-Will

Moss Phlox

Birdfoot Violet

May 1

The striking birdfoot violet is now at peak bloom. While not listed as rare or endangered in Maryland, it is unusual, and its preference for arid and rocky soils amid a human culture where such habitats are considered expendable make it a vulnerable species.

Its name is drawn from the resemblance of the finely segmented leaves to the feet of certain bird species. Other *Viola* exhibit the more familiar heart-shaped leaves.

The leafy filigree of these bird-footed plants, forming an intricate green backdrop to gorgeous purple and pale lavender five-petaled flowers poised atop tall, slender stems, is a delightful sight, especially after the long colorless winter. Additionally, the flowers often bunch together into neat oval clumps that are scattered amid the brownish, dry-leaved wood edges and rock outcrops like so many bright little islands in a dull, murky sea.

At Soldiers Delight the birdfoot violets are most numerous around Red Dog Lodge, where in places they mix nicely with the pink elegance of blooming moss phlox (*Phlox subulata*) and the whites of serpentine, or hairy field, chickweed (*Cerastium arvense* var. *villosum*) and lyre-leaved rock cress (*Arabis lyrata*). In some spots the lovely bicolored form of this violet stands out, the two "spur" petals at the flower's top being deepest ultramarine, in arresting contrast to the pale, veined trio of lower petals, many of which are speckled or blotched in delicate and whimsical ways.

Two other dry-ground species, arrow-leaved violet (*Viola*

sagittata) and ovate-leaved violet (*Viola fimbriatula*) can also be found now by the glade edges and oak copses, and the early saxifrage (*Saxifraga virginiensis*) has been visible among the rocks and dry wood margins since April, arching its white parasols of tiny flowers above a thickish, erect stem. The first hot spell will quickly wither its delicate blooms.

In another place, its exact location a well-guarded secret, that striking spring orchid, pink lady's slipper, or mocassin flower (*Cypripedium acaule*), blooms in a small colony. The semidry woods there, where trailing arbutus (*Epigaea repens*) may burst forth before the equinox, was but recently part of the serpentine, having come into loam in only the last few decades.

Elsewhere, to the west, the plantain-leaved pussytoes (*Antennaria plantaginifolia*) make their stand on the warm spring slopes. Throughout the summer and fall their silky basal leaves will adorn the hot glades and prairies, long after the flower stalks have faded.

May 3

I walked a southern circuit into the northwest sector this morning. There is an old pasture there, growing up slowly with dogwoods, maples, and other hardy colonizers. The transition is slow, largely, I believe, because of heavy deer browsing, remnant serpentine minerals, and numerous mound-building ants (subfamily *Formicinae*), who perhaps damage seedlings.

Today the whole pasture and adjacent wood edges were fragrant with a blooming shrub whose odor is like honeysuckle in its sweetness and strength. This is autumn olive, or oleaster

(*Elaeagnus umbella*), a sturdy alien ornamental that in many areas has escaped to become a pest. It has willowlike leaves, silvery below, with clusters of small white flowers that the honeybees (*Apis mellifera*), especially, are fond of.

Migrating birds, the wood warblers in particular, are now conspicuous, and reaching peak abundance. Their songs give them away, and then one can try to see them, which is often difficult. I glimpsed male and female redstarts, with their bright patches of red orange or yellow, as well as black-and-white, black-throated green, yellow-rumped, and chestnut-sided warblers, most of them in the woods and thickets near Liberty Lake.

I rested at a waterfall on Pines Branch and, from my log perch, noted blue and yellow violets, spring-beauties, jack-in-the-pulpit, skunk cabbage, three kinds of ferns, four of mosses, and many seedlings of sassafras and tulip-tree. There is nothing like a beautiful rest stop. As one relaxes and looks closely around, there may be many surprises: odd plant, insect, or artifact; strange rock, animal track, or bird's nest. For if *we* have found the place attractive, so, at some time, have our fellow creatures.

Jotting this bit of wisdom in my notebook, I arose, walked a few yards downstream to find my path, and, in an exposed bit of stream bank, extracted an odd white chunk of quartz. It looked like an arrowhead, crudely worked and broken in half diagonally—my first Indian artifact from Soldiers Delight.

May 4

This morning I was up early to bird Soldiers Delight with three other people. We logged sixty-five species in about four hours, the most unusual being northern waterthrush, black-billed cuckoo, solitary sandpiper, and golden-winged warbler. Blue-gray gnatcatchers were one of the most common, or at least most vocal, species.

In the western sector, the beautiful purple and white showy orchis (*Orchis spectablis*) were in bloom. The sparse snowy bracts of flowering dogwood bordered the deep woods, seeming, from a distance, to float upon the gloom. And the new leaves of quaking aspen (*Populus tremuloides*), here and there unfolding in silvered, feathery knots among the treetops, were oddly striking.

It is not well known that aspens occur this far south. They are usually associated with more northerly and mountainous regions, quaking aspen in particular being common in Canada and the Far West. Yet in central Maryland we have two species, the other being bigtooth aspen (*Populus grandidentata*), both noted for their color in the fall and, with their long-stemmed leaves, for the quiver and rattle of their massed foliage whenever there is wind.

May 6

Curious now about arrowheads, I searched several hours for them along Locust Run this afternoon, without success.

I did, however, meet Mr. Linthicum, whom Fraser has mentioned. I was passing under his driveway bridge, and he greeted me with suspicion, as if I were a troll. His impressive stone house, built in 1835, sits palatially back from Ward's Chapel Road, on the border of Soldiers Delight. Pestered by trespassers and even squatters (a family spent one season in his woods before being evicted), he is justifiably wary and has a reputation for testiness. My crawling about in the streambed in tattered clothes did nothing to put him at ease.

I explained myself, and we had a good chat on the bridge, at one point looking down on a black rat snake that was asleep in the branches of a tree. Given permission to explore further after we parted, I ended up at the fork of Locust Run and Chimney Branch, sweaty and tired, and without any artifacts. But there were other compensations. From a bend out of sight came faint gurglings, which I first took for voices, and which, as I emptied my mind, had the quality of prayerful babblings or incantations. A breeze rose, and rain clouds to the west were shot through with light. I sat quite still and got gooseflesh on my arms.

May 11

Today was the May Count of the Maryland Ornithological Society. Statewide birders try to see as many species and individuals as possible, in twenty-four hours. My approach is more casual than some. It was almost seven A.M. before I got out to Soldiers Delight, and I quit before noon. The northwest sector, with its fields and mixed hardwood habitats, is the most bird-rich, so I focused there.

There were few surprises in my fifty-seven total species, though I noted with interest that Kentucky warblers were singing wildly in the floodplains, when last week we heard not one. This bird, with its lovely black "sideburns" and yellow "spectacles," is especially hard to see, skulking along tangled streamsides, and running or flying through the underbrush if approached. Its song, a rapid *churry, churry, churry,* or *tootle, tootle, tootle,* resembles that of the Carolina wren, but has two syllables (*churry*) rather than the wren's usual three (*chirpity*).

Slender blue-eyed grass (*Sisyrinchium mucronatum*) was blooming beside one farm-field trail, and, in a gully at the base of a rye furrow, I found two more Indian artifacts, crudely fashioned pre-forms of a grainy, bluish quartzite.

May 12

This morning Donna and I walked the serpentine prairies directly north of the middle sector, above Ward's Chapel Road. Here slender blue-eyed grass was abundant, as was the whitish flowered serpentine chickweed, which embroidered the barest outcrops. Considerable confusion has surrounded the latter plant. In the early nineteenth century, Frederick Pursh, John Torrey, Henry Muhlenberg, Constantine Rafinesque, and William Darlington all misunderstood this rare chickweed's relation to similar species. Botanist F. W. Pennell finally sorted things out about 1930, calling the scarcest form—found only in southeast Pennsylvania—*Cerastium arvense* var. *villosissimum,* or extra hairy (sometimes long hairy) field chickweed. Despite the claim of persistent flawed records, it is *C. arvense* var. *villosum,* or hairy field chickweed, that survives today at Soldiers Delight. Both varieties are often still called serpentine chickweed, which helps preserve the muddle.

The loveliest area of our walk was a glade, somewhat north and east, hemmed by resin-scented pine groves, and awash in the hot sun with dashes of blue, white, and pink. The pink came from moss phlox, with its creeping habit and spiky leaves, that was woven in small clumps amid the chickweed and blue-eyed grass. In some serpentine regions, moss phlox forms blooming carpets so prominent that the places are nicknamed "Pink Hills." Today, from the base of one slope, it was possible to look up along the bright prairie, take in the subtle, particolored brush strokes on their canvas of rock and grass, and imagine yourself somewhere else, in some region of the arid West.

The resemblance of serpentine grasslands to parts of the American West and Midwest, has often been noted. In addition to their rockiness and aridity, they were hunted by native peoples in the manner employed by the Western tribes, that is, through the technique of "fire-hunting." The late Maryland historian William Bose Marye was a pioneering expert on both serpentine grasslands and the Native Americans who hunted them. He revealed that the Susquehannock Indians, the region's dominant tribe at the time of European settlement, made an annual or biannual pilgrimage southwest from their permanent camps along the Susquehanna River, and touched off huge rings of fire, several miles in diameter, which closed a concentric burning noose around whatever game was present, killing it outright or panicking it toward waiting bands of hunters. The prairies they hunted were in those days vast: over one hundred thousand acres in Pennsylvania alone, and extending south through Maryland to the upper Patuxent River.

The dominant grass—then, as now—which the Susquehannocks set alight, was little bluestem. This is also the chief component of the so-called short-grass prairies once common in dry regions of the West and still present there today.

It is well-adapted to heat and drought, which it meets by contracting inward the edges of its tough, narrow leaves, thus inhibiting loss of moisture.

Little bluestem conserves moisture in another, more complex way. Stomata are small pores which allow plants to take in the atmospheric carbon dioxide that, when combined with light, water, and chlorophyll within the plant, brings about photosynthesis, and thus plant growth. But if the plant's stomata were open during the scorching prairie summers, crucial water would evaporate. Little bluestem has learned to close its stomata through the burning summer days.

Yet, in order to flower and set seed by fall, it must reach its three-foot height during precisely this hot time of year. So how does it grow at all—much less a lot—when cut off from essential carbon dioxide? It seems that special enzymes within little bluestem allow it to photosynthesize even with closed stomata. Aided by these chemicals, it makes extra-efficient use of what little carbon dioxide is absorbed—mostly during the short summer nights—when the pores are partly open. These, then, are the tactics of a true zerophyte, which is adapted both inside and out for thriving in very dry places.

Little bluestem matures in autumn. It is mostly the skeletons of last year's plants, buffy and insubstantial, that vertically stripe the glades now, pallid in the vernal light, quaking faintly in the breezes amid varied pastel blooms.

May 15

I birded and botanized at Soldiers Delight this sunny morning, with our neighbor, John Smith. For a man almost seventy, with a heart condition, he is a game hiker, very enthusiastic about every aspect of nature. He grew up in Highlandtown, one of the most naturally depleted inner sections of Baltimore, which makes his interest all the more surprising. Or maybe it doesn't. My own love of nature was whetted by the crowded monotonies of a suburban Chicago childhood.

In the evening I listened for whip-poor-wills and chuck-wills-widows at the overlook. Soldiers Delight is one of the few places around where "whips," as well as "chucks," can be heard. Whip-poor-wills were once common rurally, but habitat loss greatly reduced them, while chuck-will's-widows are birds more common to the Coastal Plain. Having both species at a single Piedmont location, and only miles from a metropolis, is a true oddity.

I heard the first chuck just at dusk, about 8:30. The "chuck" prefix is often inaudible, so the call becomes *will-widow! will-widow!* But noise from pickups, motorcycles, and lover's-lane parkers drove me elsewhere. At a spot off Ward's Chapel Road, I heard one whip that called nonstop, and very loudly, for three and a half minutes. A fellow birder, Dave Walbeck, tells me this is nothing. Indeed, the late Hal Borland, in *Hill Country Harvest*, relates hearing a sequence of 564 calls, while John Burroughs once counted 1,300 straight recitals of what sounds like *whip-poor-weeill!* At about a second per call, this works out to almost ten minutes for the Borland bird, and over twenty-one for the Burroughs. It's not surprising that the bird is sometimes disliked for keeping people awake.

May 16

This morning I went hunting for projectile points along Pines Branch. An arc of rye fields slopes down to where it begins as two deep gullies forking together from the hillside. The high, eroded banks reveal centuries of soil. I tried to ignore the trash heaps at the start and focused on the streambed. Sun pierced down through huge tulip-trees, whose orange blossoms glowed in the canopy or floated in the purling current. Rocks and gravel glistened; verdant vines covered all but midstream. At one point a great trunk base was undercut to a height above my head, where, when parted, the dangling curtain of rootlets revealed a cool chamber with sinewed ceilings and walls and a dark pool for a floor. Here I captured a northern dusky salamander (*Desmognathus fuscus fuscus*), shiny with brown and flinty gray, and who I soon turned back to the tinted pool.

Farther downstream was perhaps the prettiest eastern box turtle (*Terrapene carolina carolina*) I've ever seen, streaked on head and legs with broad slashes of chrome yellow, its carapace painted likewise, in bright enamel flashes.

I found nothing Indian for two hours. Then I pulled a tusk-like piece of amber quartz from the bank, and had my first whole arrowhead. Modest finds came quickly after that. Most were mere fragments, flakes, and pre-forms—the latter roughed-out preliminary pieces that could later be worked into points—but I stuck them all in my bag and sorted them out at home.

May 19

The bow and arrow did not come to eastern North America until about 800 A.D., beginning a period that archeologists call Late Woodland. It replaced, or in some cases supplemented, the *atlatl,* a powerful jointed spear thrower that could hurl missiles hundreds of feet. For almost eleven thousand years—from the end of the last Ice Age to our recent millennium of tribal archers—spears and atlatls ruled. By sheer force of time in production, then, most eastern points were atlatl spear points, and most were turned out from about 8,000 B.C. to 1,000 B.C., the so-called Archaic period.

Meanwhile, when Europeans arrived, the dominant nomads of the Soldiers Delight region were the Piscataway and Susquehannock tribes. About 1600 the once-powerful Piscataways were succumbing to a long feud that had driven them permanently south of the Patapsco River. To the north, the apparent victors in this feud, the Susquehannocks, made frequent punitive raids southward to the Patapsco and below. In short, both tribes often passed through the prairied "White Grounds" of Soldiers Delight, to camp briefly near the Patapsco while hunting and warring. Large game was killed by deliberate fire-hunting, but smaller game, like turkeys and pigeons, were abundant, and no doubt the most frequent targets.

So how do Late Woodland peoples, harassed by each other, forever on the move, and surrounded by abundant small game, make arrowheads? Fairly quickly. Fine craftsmanship wasn't needed when passenger pigeons, as even white settlers recalled, collapsed trees with their combined weight and blackened the sky in flight. Indeed it was counterproductive in a temporary camp, with murderous enemies nearby, to toy and fuss with tools whose chief function was to kill easy game. And if, when looking for stone materials, you found a lot of other objects, like lost and broken points from your Archaic forebears, you could easily use or resharpen those.

In fact the finest points I have seen, in several private collections, date mainly from the Archaic period: carefully flaked or ground pieces of rhyolite and milky quartz, deeply notched and stemmed. They are graceful works of art. Perhaps the art reached its zenith then. By Late Woodland times, in this area, the styles were often simpler, the work cruder. Constant warfare, especially late in the epoch, and the need to improvise and keep moving in the face of it, may explain this.

Whatever the reason, such crudeness has its place. In every craft there are degrees of workmanship, and while some don't impress collectors, there is still much they can tell us. I'm not looking for museum-quality artifacts, merely confirmation of tribal activity in the area, so each piece, finished or not, is a clue to Indian presence and has a value all its own.

May 21

This morning I found my first truly "identifiable" point, that is, one which clearly resembled a type described in *Stone Age Spear and Arrow Points of the Midcontinental and Eastern United States,* by Noel Justice. I had searched Mill Run for a change, which proved more productive than Pines Branch. I was able to classify the point only at home, when I'd cleaned it and looked at my books. I believe it's the unfinished bottom half of a white quartzite spear point, Savannah River Cluster, a Late Archaic piece from about 2000 B.C.

Whether or not I find artifacts, my journeys along the stream bank have become satisfying adventures. Today I moved with calm and deliberation, pleasantly alert for a familiar shape or type of stone, while all about me, with a second level of awareness, I noted bird songs (most prominently, pine and parula warblers, Baltimore oriole, scarlet tanager, Louisiana waterthrush, and pileated woodpecker), and with a third level sensed all else—the harmony of colors, odors, cool drafts, sky glimpses, water gurgles, and endless light-pierced greenery; the unity of a natural oasis so nicely shut apart from man. Yet I was looking for things man-made. Man being what he is, I suppose to me his residue is often more attractive that his reality.

May 22

This afternoon I explored Red Run, in the eastern sector. I found no artifacts by the stream bank. Hemmed in more by dry glades and barrens, the place is full of serpentinite, brittle material unsuitable for points. I did get a good look at a male Kentucky warbler, who came out of hiding to challenge me with his loud *tchip!* alarm note. These birds nest near the ground, and I must have almost stepped on his for all the anger he displayed.

The close proximity of both soapstone (or steatite) and quartzite at Soldiers Delight may be archeologically significant. William Henry Holmes, working for the Smithsonian Institution in 1890, found soapstone quarries near the Potomac River, just forty miles to our south. The soapstone was quarried by native peoples in the so-called Late Archaic period, using quartzite tools, which were also mined nearby. Additionally, quartzite tools were used to scrape out the center of steatite bowls, in the epochs before clay pottery. Roughly shaped picks, axes, and gouges—many crude ones broken or rejected in the making—were collected in the hundreds by Holmes.

Some of these quartz oddities resemble those I have found. Many more such articles are probably scattered through this area, or were collected years ago, and reside in private collections. Indeed, one old-timer of the Soldiers Delight neighborhood recalls shards of soapstone pottery being plowed up by his farming relations, who then discarded them in a nearby stream!

May 24

I got my canoe down to the Locust Run cove just before dawn. The beaver met me right away. Once again, fishing in the cove itself became useless amid all their percussions.

Instead I tried an experiment. I took a tiny split-shot, pinched it onto my line, and dropped the line to the bottom in the very center of the cove. The lake level is high, as high as I've ever known it. After years of droughty springtimes, we've had wet springs the last two years, and this year rain has been ample right into May. The cove is so full that several landmarks on the bank have been drowned. Coincidentally, the DNR recently found striped bass, or rockfish (*Morone saxatilis*), to be breeding here for the first time. So they set up a closed season to protect this new development among a major Maryland game fish.

What has this got to do with my line? Traditionally, striped bass move from salt water up fresh-water rivers to spawn. For the two or three days it takes the eggs to hatch, the water must not only be fresh, but flowing. Eggs sinking to the bottom die. Thus in static man-made impoundments, where the bass have been heavily stocked, reproduction is rare. Except, I have theorized, when lake levels and spring rains are sufficient to keep streams flowing a good distance, long enough for a two-day gestation. But these fish are in a lake. What streams am I referring to? Well, the streams that flow under the lake, toward the dam. The fingery coves of all reservoirs represent stream channels, and the beds of those channels, though narrow, still "flow" under all that water in sufficiently wet seasons. Even as the beaver slapped their tails in the cove around me, the thin monofilament eight feet below was drifting, however slowly, in the "current" of Locust Run, toward the center of Liberty Lake. Which is really the Patapsco River. Which is one reason why striped bass can breed here. I think.

But my problem was how to catch them. I tied on my recycled Jitterbug, left the main cove, and fished the quiet shoreline in failure for half an hour. Then I put on a big balsa wood minnow and twitched it around on the surface in what I recognized as the cove of Pines Branch. The sun was just at the treetops, the last mist was melting, and the lake so quiet that the faint lisp of a black-and-white warbler could be heard on the other bank. Soon a big fish slurped my lure under and I snapped the line taut. It jumped several times before I brought it in—not a striper—but a largemouth bass (*Micropterus salmoides*) that measured sixteen inches and topped two pounds. More to the point, here was a shining creature grown up beyond the sight of man, and revealed now for the first time—a visitor from another realm, breaking wildly into my world. I could hear that familiar spirit, the waterthrush, singing loudly to the east. Probably near the waterfall, I mused, where I found that first broken point.

The beaver had gone to bed when I worked back to Locust Run, and couldn't have known my success. Childish, I admit, but I gave them a little nose-thumb as I passed by their lodge.

May 27

Another unseasonably warm day. I started early into the northwest sector, tape measure in hand, intent on measuring the big sycamore. I walked around to its low side above the spring and found, at chest height on the trunk, where I needed to begin, a four-foot black rat snake. Attached in an S-curve, quite perpendicular to the ground, it wouldn't budge, and proved hard to dislodge when proded. Black rat snakes achieve this grip by wedging their belly scales into fissures and cracks in the bark. They are at home not merely *in* trees, but *on* them, as it were, even at unlikely angles.

Finally, with utter composure and grace, the snake glided down to the spring, kept its head alertly cocked toward me, and found a crevice in the rocks where it virtually melted from sight. I was full of admiration. The snake had upstaged my measurement, but the tree's circumference of twenty-five feet, two inches, was still rather impressive.

I followed the creek that issues from the spring, to its junction with Mill Run. Then I worked upstream, keeping an eye out for artifacts. But there were other things of interest. Jack-in-the-pulpit, those more delicate kin of skunk cabbage, are now in full bloom, though the blooms are but a few small flowers hidden low on the spadix. This phalluslike spadix, or "jack," is itself shrouded by the greenish spathe, and "preacher Jack" is said to be in his "pulpit" at this time of year. I was surprised to find one of these odd plants, normally anchored in the loamy floodplain, grown tall in four inches of water near midstream.

Another surprise was a periodical cicada (*Magicicada* species), a just-emerged adult with red eyes and wing-veins, and a black body. These are the so-called seventeen-year ci-cada, but as we just saw them emerge four years ago, I was puzzled. Perhaps a few individuals hatch out of sync with the others, and show up several years late. It also seems possible that regional cycles among subspecies or races can overlap slightly, and a few stragglers may be blown off course from broods north or south.

Spiderwort (*Tradescantia virginiana*) is blooming in the floodplain. Its leaves remind me of iris, though the flat, three-petaled blue flowers are anything but irislike. Exploring fur-ther, by accident I crossed north of Mill Run, and came upon a piney hillside littered with the large hillocks of mound-building ants. At over a dozen spots the reddish dirt was piled two feet high in flat cones, and the big red-and-black ants scurried everywhere beneath me, so that even if I stopped for an instant they careened over my shoe-tops. Knowing how sharply they can bite, I kept moving.

Thus went the morning—so full of small diversions that a single focus was difficult. I did find one worn artifact—the pre-form of a quartz projectile point—but the lingering sense of discovery was made rounder and fuller by the natural rich-ness around me.

June *Amber Light and Shadow*

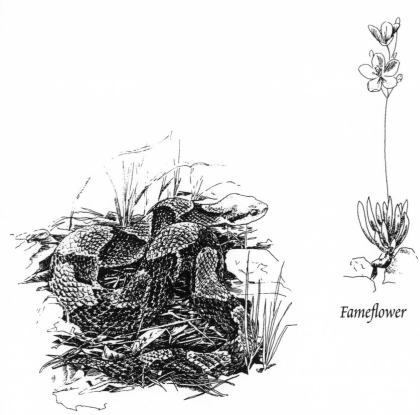

Northern Copperhead

Fameflower

Edwards Hairstreak

June 1

Summer is suddenly here—well ahead of the calendar—for the days are blazingly hot. In the morning Donna and I walked the eastern sector and found many wildflowers, including the tiny Deptford pink (*Dianthus armeria*), which is common near the Choate Mine. This species, though not rare, linked with serpentine, or even native, is showy in its lilliputian way, the small flower coming close to what some call hot pink in the world of commercial fashion.

Bordering the rocky trails were several species of daisies (family *Compositae*), with both white and yellow petals, and mints (family *Labiatae*)—especially heal-all (*Prunella vulgaris*)—in shades from pink to purple, grown up even in the trails themselves. Bluets were still in bloom, some with five petals, and blossoms of serpentine, or hairy field, chickweed ranged from white to pink.

Hairy field chickweed has adapted to the often searing temperatures in the barrens by evolving very fuzzy leaves and stems. Hair or fuzz, termed "pubescence" by botanists, is a common plant adaptation to heat and dryness. It helps to capture and hold moisture, even the ephemeral moisture of humid air, while the dense layers of short whitish filaments reduce evaporation and reflect bright sunlight that would otherwise scorch the plant.

One of the commonest warm weather serpentine flowers is sundrops (*Oenothera* species), a day-blooming form of evening-primrose that is often mistaken for the latter. At least two species exist at Soldiers Delight, though their highly variable foliage makes them hard to clearly identify. The bright yellow flowers, with orange stamens, were today cupped against the heat atop tall lance-leaved stems.

A phenomenon of the neighboring savannas and woodlands is young oaks with huge leaves sometimes one foot across. This is apparently a tactic—not limited to oaks—for catching more sunlight on the shaded forest floor. Thus a small tree can hang on in arrested youth, till the death of one older makes room.

Other species exploit scarce forest light, as evidenced by a patch of blackberry (*Rubus allegheniensis*), fully eight feet tall, that had filled a gap left by dead oaks. The trees were probably victims of gypsy moths (*Porthetria dispar*). Especially in the eastern sector, damage from these moths is considerable, and conspicuous amid the present lushness, when bare limbs and branches stand out from afar.

Returning to our car we found a purplish clump of everlasting pea (*Lathyrus latifolius*) by the roadside, its pealike leaves and tendrils tangled beside the gravel.

June 3

Before the heat took over this morning, I explored the eastern prairie glades of the northwest sector. Once again there was Deptford pink near the roadway. On the baking slopes, lyre-leaved rock cress, with its thin, spiky pods on unlovely stems, rose above the bluets. The rock cress has now been in bloom for well over a month, in some places bunching in many-branched, herby mounds, a foot or two high, their tops spangled with the four-petaled flowers that typify all members of the mustard family.

Lyre-leaved rock cress might better be named "lute-leaved rock cress," for the basal rosettes of scalloped green leaves remind one not of lyres, which are harp-shaped instruments, but rather the necks of the guitarlike lute, their deep, even-spaced lobes resembling crude tuning pegs. These rosettes remain on the ground through most of the year, even when the stalky upper foliage has collapsed, appearing like tiny sundials in the soil, or perhaps a kind of medallion, changing their hue with the seasons, from chrome green to absinthe, to cordovan or henna, to nearly bronze in winter. Their little coinage scatters the glades, awaiting the emblem of the new year's warmth, the fresh minting of the springtime sun.

The deep yellow small's ragwort (*Senecio anonymous*), a daisy species rare elsewhere in Maryland, is everywhere now in the prairies, along with many sundrops.

Prairie warblers spiraled their rising songs, rufous-sided towhees *chewinked,* and in a small rocky depression I found the unusual fameflower (*Talinum teretifolium*). This member of the purslane family has a deep pink five-petaled flower and bright green succulent leaves whorled tightly at its base. These leaves, which are faintly translucent in strong light, help to store moisture through the hot, dry summer. As early as 1804, the eccentric naturalist Constantine Rafinesque mentions finding fameflower near West Chester, Pennsylvania, on some "singular magnesian rocks," which were undoubtedly serpentinite. These days it is rare and threatened in Maryland, and elsewhere. Unseasonable heat and drought seems to have hastened its appearance this year, but from now until early September it will continue to produce its vivid flowers atop threadlike stems. Yet even in summer it blooms but briefly each day, usually in the hottest hours.

This afternoon I chanced to read the recent *Sun* story on Berry's Hill, by our visiting reporter of April. It confirmed my worst suspicions. "Nature Center Shares Turf with Ax-Murder Hanging" and "Gruesome Past Haunts Nature Center" were the headlines, while the piece stated flatly that "the new center is atop Berry's Hill" and "it was here that John Berry was hanged and his body left to rot." There was no hint of doubt, no mention that the sentence was to be carried out "on the highest point near the scene of the commission of the crime," which, according to maps that the reporter himself examined in our presence, is *not* beside the Visitor Center, nor even on the same hill. Based on the only reliable evidence outside hearsay, Berry's Hill is most likely the one to the north, and at the least, is of uncertain location.

Disregarding all this, the publicity advantage of linking a nature center with a grisly murder and hanging is difficult to see. But I suppose it does sell newspapers.

June 7

The dry weather continues. I hiked the cooler northwest sector this morning. Along Mill Run was a pleasant smell of wild mint and that nostalgic, ineffable mustiness of all wet places. During a brief artifact search I turned up what I think are two Indian "T" drills—small, T-shaped stone drilling implements that were held with thumb and forefinger. For the first time I noticed that some of the jewelweed (*Impatiens capenis*) in the streambed has stem bases of translucent purple. This species, also called touch-me-not, is related to the cultivated pastel "impatiens" of urban gardens, and, in its orange- or yellow-blossomed late summer glory, will perform the same trick: disgorging sprays of seeds when ripe pods are touched.

I drank my coffee on a big fallen tree that spans the stream. Nearby there were many black-winged damselflies (*Calopteryx maculata*)—six near a single sandbar—as well as the slower, fluttering dobsonflies (*Corydalus* species), drifting through light and shadow or perching above the water.

A family of white-breasted nuthatches was about, which confirmed them as breeders for my bird list, and I watched them dart from tree to tree, squeaking and yanking peevishly.

My log perch itself was adorned with common split gills (*Schizophyllum commune*)—gray, leathery fungi attached to the outer wood like fluted sprays of coral. Beside my left leg, ants were crossing back and forth on the bridge, but paying me no mind. Red and black, they looked like the big mound-builders that so dominate the woodland floor nearby. Meanwhile, I dropped crumbs from my blueberry muffin to the pool below. Minnows and dace attacked these as they sank, or nipped them off the surface. Nuthatches yanked from afar, titmice and cardinals whistled, goldfinches twittered overhead, while the stream burbled faintly and danced with reflections.

At one point on the trail back I noted great bowers of wild grape (*Vitis* species) and American bittersweet (*Celastris scandens*), thirty feet aloft, blotting out the sun. One of the grape stems was wrist-thick at its base. Even a vine only two inches broad, if cut in a six-foot section, is said to yield two cups of clear, drinkable liquid. Grape is thus a capable tree-killer, blocking light at the crown while stealing water from the roots.

I stopped once more at the great sycamore, where carrion

beetles (*Silpha* species) fed leisurely on a nearby mound of fox scat. Then, while I cleared some leaves from the rock-walled spring, I noticed behind me that, true to his promise, Fraser Bishop has removed the big oil drum from midstream.

June 10

This morning I took the clay pipe fragment and 1835 large cent over to Ranger Bishop. I'm hoping these will make part of an interesting display at the new Visitor Center, and in any case they rightly belong to Soldiers Delight. I also showed him the Indian artifacts, but these will need further verification.

As I was driving along his winding gravel road, I saw an eastern hog-nosed snake (*Heterodon platyrhinos*) crossing just ahead of me. I stopped and got out to watch a colorful yard-long creature, with yellow orange blotches among brown and black, move slowly into the dry underbrush past the shoulder. The black rat snake is more conspicuous at Soldiers Delight but is chiefly a woodland species, while the hog-nosed likes dry fields, scrub, and open woods where its favorite morsels are toads. Though harmless, hog-noseds stage elaborate bluffs, hissing, flattening their heads, and puffing up with air. Their bluff called, they generally roll over like the family dog, gape their mouths, and play dead. If at all possible they will soon slink away. Yet people in love with snake-fear have labeled them "blow viper" and "puff adder," preferring myth to reality.

After this encounter I hiked up by the old Ware Mill in the northwest corner, where Mill Run nears the reservoir and there is a lush wooded hollow. Rock walls and ledges, hoary with moss, pinch the stream into low cascades that then bleed out into pools. In one of these I found a mottled sculpin (*Cottus bairdi*), a bug-eyed little fish with primitive fins that was darting about in the silt. A belted kingfisher rattled nearby and a parula warbler buzzed. Kentucky warblers and ovenbirds called, a Louisiana waterthrush gurgled, and the commonest bird in the summer eastern woodlands, the drab red-eyed vireo, pursued its monotonous song.

One of the commonest *brilliant* bird in these warm-weather forests is, to the average person, the least expected and appreciated. Scarlet tanagers, in stunning plumage of crimson and black, arrive from South America in May and pair off in most fair-size tracts of hardwood. To many who have glimpsed them up close they must seem an exotic bird. Yet any Breeding Bird Survey—a mostly auditory census conducted at dawn by expert birders in cars—would be flawed if more than a few big woods were passed without this species being heard. The casual weekend hiker hears them in the forest all summer, yet knows not what he hears. Even if actually glimpsed, in the deep gloom of the canopy, or backlighted against the sky, their red looks merely dark, and the male's song is a raspy robin- or vireolike repetition. Thus, like many wild beauties, they carry on—as one did today beyond the dripping pools—barely noticed by humans, their shy carols muted in the treetops and their brilliance lost to shadow.

June 12

I walked the dry middle sector this afternoon, as a weak front has brought cooler air. Great spangled fritillaries (*Speyeria cybele*) are now conspicuous, beating strongly along the trails and barren lanes. Cardinals, rufous-sided towhees, prairie warblers, and common yellowthroats were the perverse children of the undergrowth here, being heard but not seen. Much lichen and moss covers the arid ground between the outcrops, with pyxie cups and British Soldiers most visible. Hunks of rust-hued, deeply pocked limonite (hydrous iron oxide) littered my path, a cottontail limped in the grass, and field crickets chirped. Both Deptford pink and bright yellow small's ragwort were plentiful, overflown in jagged sorties by narrow-winged damselflies (family *Coenagrionidae*).

In a field just north of Fraser's place is the stone cellar of an old log cabin, which was once the office of a mining company, and later part of a two-story house. Originally constructed entirely of American chestnut logs, the cabin was burned down by vandals several years ago, leaving only this tiny basement. Now, hemmed by sumacs, mints, grasses, and vines, it is frequented by foxes. Their droppings were everywhere along the broken rim, and were full of the pits of cherries. Yet what cherry fruits this early? I pondered this as I sat on the brink and looked down on the tangled basement, wondering too what creatures might colonize such an overgrown structure. Bright afternoon is not the time to discover them.

Moving on I found common milkweed (*Asclepias syriaca*) near to blooming, and much Queen Anne's lace (*Daucus carota*). A weedy junk pile has been tunneled under, first no doubt by woodchucks, and later by those frequent usurpers of woodchuck homes, the red foxes. Fox scat and prey litter, especially feathers, are now strewn by the entrance. Not far down the sloping tunnel the wheeled bottom corner of a metal cabinet was visible, blocking almost half the way.

Finally, in a field, I came upon the fragments of a box turtle carapace. Another mystery. What local animal could so break apart this shell, which is as hard as the hardest plastic? Not the red fox. A nimble raccoon might make the kill, but could it break this armor in pieces? Yet flesh, even connecting tissue, had been scraped thoroughly from the inside of the shell by some living thing.

I was reminded how hungry wild animals can get, and of how hard are their lives. The myth of the "peaceable kingdom," where all creatures coexist happily in some Ark-like Eden, is of course just that: a total myth. Yet our commercial culture is rife with peaceable kingdom notions. What most people crave is not science but sentimentality, as witness the great popularity of Disney animation and its endless imitations, wherein anthropomorphic mice or ducks in shorts or toddler attire confront their problems like tiny humans, and shout and laugh and weep their way to happy endings.

In real nature, all living things, including man, are out for their own self-interest at the expense of any who can nourish them, and all their highly evolved strengths are at one time or another turned toward this end. Such competition is usually so basic and unrelenting that they do not merely differ with their neighbors but attempt to dislodge them and wear them down, and then often kill and eat them. In the case of plants, who are no exception, the deed is done very slowly, by strangulation or engulfment, then absorption of their decayed neighbors through their roots.

What is left between times, for most life forms, is the solace of what we would call ignorance, while for us large-brained types there is the endlessly variable balm of illusion.

June 14

Hot and still. In the eastern sector, near the parking lot east of Deer Park Road, I briefly heard what sounded like a red-breasted nuthatch: a squeaky, double-noted *neet-neet*. I tried to call the bird up, but all was then silence. The piney habitat here would suit a breeding pair, though finding them this far east of the mountains in summer would be a great rarity.

Further on, at the entrance to the Choate Mine, the nest of an eastern phoebe was attached to a ledge fully ten feet inside the rock overhang. The nest was empty, and there were no signs of parent birds.

Drought and heat are tightening their grip. Beside the trail the blossoms of Carolina rose, or pasture rose (*Rosa carolina*), are already drying up, and many of the buds have been bored through by insects seeking moisture and sustenance.

Just to the south, an old pit about eight feet deep, which was full of water and frog eggs several months ago, is quite dry, as are other wet spots and basins. Near one I found the dinnerplate-size carapace of a snapping turtle (*Chelydra serpentina*). This reptile was probably forced to abandon its pool, then caught in the open by a predator.

In the arid groves, hollow, walnut-size oak galls—often called oak apple galls—hang from the leaves of blackjack oak (*Quercus marilandica*), their small holes being evidence of gall wasps (family *Cynipinae*), who grow and pupate within before exiting as adults. Galls themselves appear where disease or insect larvae form constant irritation on bark or leaves, causing a protective sheath of cell matter to erupt at the point of injury, a bit like cysts in mammals. In some cases the gall wasps themselves cause the galls to form, in others they merely inhabit galls made by other organisms.

The open glades between these groves support many Virginia pine, stunted to six feet tall and less, yet maturely displaying a half-dozen cones or more. Such stunting is a unique feature of the dry and poisonous barrens. The smallest mature pine I could find was just three and a half feet tall, with four well-formed cones.

Distinct, dwarf tree species also exist at Soldiers Delight, including the eastern dwarf cherry (*Prunus susquehanae*), and the prairie dwarf willow (*Salix humilis* var. *microphylla*). The latter can be found along streams in the serpentine regions, assuming a low, herblike habit, compact and bushy, with gray green and slightly roughened—not densely hairy (as described by some field guides)—twigs and leaves.

On my way back I found the little wood satyr (*Euptychia cymela*). A subtle butterfly of browns and grays, with four eyelike spots edging its wings, it fluttered just off the ground in the thin shade by the trail.

June 17

The mystery of the cherry pits in the fox dung is solved. The endemic eastern dwarf cherry might first have been suspected, but in fact that species fruits rather late—usually in August—and the pits of its blackish cherries are small. Instead I discovered that the only wild cherry with fair-size pits that fruits in early June is the sour cherry (*Prunus cerasus*), a shrublike alien whose berries may be clustered on low spur branches, thus making them accessible, while still on their stems, to hungry foxes.

June 18

The drought was broken slightly by light morning rain. I went in search of those phantom red-breasted nuthatches. Phantom, indeed, they are, for I saw or heard no more sign of them, despite repeating my *neet-neet* call throughout the copses of pine.

What I did find were many of the typical animals and plants of the summer groves and glade edges. Hooded warblers, more commonly birds of the Coastal Plain, are comfortable here, and the male's distinctive *weeta-weeta-weet-see-o!*, which I mimicked with a call of my own, led me close to a breeding pair. Another pair attracted to my calls, two indigo buntings, showed up with their fledged young beside them.

What scarlet tanagers are to the summer hardwood forests—that is, common but little-noticed birds of great brilliance—so indigo buntings are to rural field edges and brushy borders. Instead of scarlet, the males flash vibrant blue, yet which, like the tanager's colors, often seems simply dark from a distance or when backlighted by the sun. Males festoon fences and utility wires along most country roads but are largely ignored by humans rushing to and fro. Like the tanagers, females are drab (brown as opposed to dull green), suggesting some humble sparrow, and the bunting's song, too, is undistinguished, a persistent jumble of warblerlike phrases that does not invite discovery. The male of this particular family briefly kept up his tune while deftly changing perches.

Ovenbirds, red- and white-eyed vireos, Acadian flycatchers, and, of course, prairie warblers, were also vocal. Silence will settle in July, as young are fledged and nests abandoned; by August some species will begin heading south.

There is much blueberry amid these groves, and the sweetish berries, frosted with pale powder and full of tiny seeds, are now coming ripe. Several varieties of these members of the heath family are evident; a few may in fact be crosses. Young bushes are hard to classify anyway, but in this stunting shade and soil, where the species have hybridized for centuries, the task is especially daunting. Yet at least two are widespread species and have been positively identified by Sara Tangren of the University of Maryland. One is a true blueberry, *Vaccinium stamineum*, often called deerberry, which has two distinct leaf sizes on the same plant, the smaller being actually a leafy bract. Another species is *Gaylussacia baccata,* or black huckleberry. Huckleberry leaves, when held to the light, show tiny resinous dots, and the berries themselves contain about ten small chambers where seeds develop, while the true blueberries have but five such chambers.

The oaks here, too, are hard to identify. Many trees, like my blackjack oak with the apple galls, display typical leaves: shallowly three-lobed at their wide apex, say, or, like the post oak (*Quercus stellata*)—that other common savanna species— deeply five-lobed. Yet many others combine characteristics of both species, especially in the leaves, which are further altered by age and health. Still a third similar species, scrub, or bear, oak (*Quercus ilicifolia*) adds to the problem. So once again various factors, especially hybridization, often confound certainty.

June 20

I read today an account of vacationing canoeists on a wilderness river in Canada. Though professing communion with nature, they spent the better part of six weeks outdoing each other with exertion, covering long distances each day, then complaining of exhaustion and quarrels. Little wonder. What could they really *see* of nature at twenty miles a day, battling like gladiators for reputations of strength. One square mile scrutiny of that wilderness, or any other, would delight a keen observer for a week, and have nothing of frenzy about it. Better yet to explore one's own state or county, not in the obvious places, but in those out of the way that take patience just to find. There are half a lifetime of natural discoveries in any good size park, and you need not be strong or quick to uncover them. In fact it's often better if you're not. Quiet, alertness, and a responsive heart are the keys, while haste is decidedly a drawback. The French entomologist J. Henri Fabre, whom many consider one of the great naturalists of all time, spent twenty-eight years examining the life-forms on a dry patch of land less than three acres in size. About this lilliputian world he composed nine accurate, surprising, and highly readable volumes of prose, containing more than 2,500 pages and over 800,000 words.

June 24

Sunny and warm. The first annual cicada, or dogday harvestflies (*Tibicen canicularis*) are singing their old sad songs. I got out to the eastern sector about midmorning, and found my first pitch pine (*Pinus rigida*) on the edge of the prairies. Unlike the far more common Virginia pine, its needles are attached to the twigs in "bundles" of three, not two, and are slightly longer as well. Its branches appear fuller and fluffier, and an especially distinctive feature is needle-clusters growing directly from the trunk, all the way to the ground and even just below it. The species has chunky, reddish maroon bark plates, or scales.

I am still looking for table mountain pine (*Pinus pungens*), the scarcest of the three dry-country pines at Soldiers Delight. Normally found on arid slopes of the Appalachian range, it is similar to pitch and Virginia pine, but, among other differences, its egg-shaped, spike-tipped cones appear in clusters, not ones or twos.

Common wood nymphs (*Cercyonis pegala*) were about, as was a delicate coral hairstreak (*Harkenclenus titus*), the region's only *tailless* hairstreak butterfly. Another hairstreak butterfly, Edwards hairstreak (*Satyrium edwardsii*), inhabits these same glades, and is rare elsewhere in the state, and indeed anywhere south of Pennsylvania. Its larvae feed exclusively on scrub and post oak, while adults prefer the nectar of certain milkweeds and goldenrods.

At Soldiers Delight an unusual symbiotic relationship exists between this rare butterfly and the nearby mound-builder ants. The larvae of the Edwards hairstreak secrete a syrupy liquid that the ants enjoy. Meanwhile, the proximity of these aggressive ants discourages parasitic wasps and other carnivorous insects that might otherwise threaten the caterpillars. This is the essence of symbiosis. In this case, both ants and caterpillars—quite dissimilar organisms—benefit together, though in different ways, from their close association in the dry glades of Soldiers Delight.

Another rare invertebrate that appears here is *Polypleurus perforatus*, a member of the tenebrionid beetle family, sometimes called "darkling beetles." It is most common in the deeper South, but occurs here under dead-fall and tree litter, on the dry wooded margins of serpentine. A tidy landscape will doom it. Sanitized farm yards, cleaned and raked wood edges, or overly thorough firewood collection, have removed this and other darkling beetles from some regions. Like many inhabitants of the wild, it depends on wood litter for shelter and food, on the windfall opulence of self-pruned trees, and on the random messiness of tree growth, death, and decay.

June 27

Hot summer weather. I hiked to the west end of northwest sector and worked my way back upstream along Pines Branch. The hardwood canopy there is now densely green overhead, the air thick with a pleasant, almost tropical, moistness and vegetable aroma. Where sunlight penetrates, it is fractured by thick branches, suffusing them to emerald while it glints down and parquets the gurgling streambed with amber light and shadow.

It was cooler here. I found chanterelle waxy caps (*Hygrophorus cantharellus*)—orange, umbrellalike mushrooms—on the log where I once watched the water striders, and a worm-eating warbler was very vocal, often repeating its cicadalike song from a hidden, shifting location. Skunk cabbage leaves are now big, dull, tattered, and broken, and—as I penned these adjectives in my notebook—reminded me comically of aging human beings.

The worm-eating warbler circled me in his buzzing explorations, and indeed the whole woodland seemed more enveloping at this season, more engulfing, and very much larger in size. The sheer act of movement and penetration was harder. I enjoyed proceeding slowly, stepping with care to this mossy rock and that glistening gravel bar. It was easy to imagine the fairly recent past—a geologic time-speck of three hundred years—when wolves, cougar, bear, and elk moved about here, and came to such streams to drink.

The junglelike verdure, especially the profusion of streamside ferns, and the rank humidity, made me think also of reptiles, and at that very moment I saw on a sandbar ahead of me an uncoiled, motionless snake. A quick study of its triangular head, hourglass markings, and thickish middle body convinced me it was a northern copperhead (*Agkistrodon contortrix*). These are rare and shy in the area, and as it was a small specimen, I decided it would make an excellent attraction at the Visitor Center. I resolved to capture it.

I had my small, red day-pack, but noticed there were two sizeable holes in the main chamber. Only the small zippered side pouch would be suitable. I broke off a forked branch and, as the snake had still not moved, worked this slowly behind its head and gently pinned it to the sand. It was utterly docile, as copperheads often are. I grasped it behind the head, lifted it with care, lowered it tail first into the pouch, then quickly released it with a downward thrust and slid the zipper across. The walk back to my car was as fast as I could reasonably make it, to minimize any heat stress to my captive.

June 28

Hot and humid. Fraser tells me that the opening of the Visitor Center has been delayed at least several months, due to lack of staff and money, so he can't use the copperhead. It spent the night at the Irvine Natural Science Center in Stevenson, where the naturalist Keith Harrison kindly took it in.

I decided the snake should be returned, to the exact spot at which I found it. This afternoon, with it safely suspended in a stiff plastic bag, I walked it back to the west end of Pines Branch. On the same sandbar where I'd kidnapped it yesterday, it emerged from the bag slowly and calmly, as though nothing had transpired in the interim. I was charmed by its facile grace, how it moved with little effort as if floating a bit off the ground. Its blotchy patterns of cinnamon on buff both blended and clashed with the surroundings, and it paused to raise its tubelike neck, carrying at right angles the compact, delicate head, which was shaped like a tricornered pendant. The topside of this locket was pale and finely stippled, suggesting worked copper or gold, and minutely edged with black and citrine along the jaw line, the eyes small beads of amber halved by ebony slits. Otherworldly in its movements, jewel-like in both appointments and scarcity, its total effect was striking, almost supernatural, as of some necklace or finely wrought amulet that was brought to life by a sorcerer. While sun shafts streamed down through the hot jade canopy, it slipped from sight beneath a broken frond of skunk cabbage.

The embankment opposite the sandbar, I now noticed, was the same where I found my first arrowhead fragment in early May. A few yards further upstream was my waterfall rest stop of last winter and spring. The "falls," though reduced by drought to a half-dozen trickles, were still hypnotic, and I sat beside them on a mossy log, took off shoes and socks, put my water-bottle of iced-coffee against a rock in the pool, and soaked my feet in the cool silty sand. The ooze that I worked through my toes was full of mica flakes that, when I lifted my coated feet, shone in the dappled sunlight like gold dust. A huge black and rust eastern crayfish (*Cambarus bartoni*), maybe five inches long, stalked a deep ledge in the pool, and raccoon prints were plain along the muddy bank. I drank my coffee and watched a lovely butterfly, the common blue (*Celastrina argiolus*) land briefly on my sweaty castoff sock.

Refreshed and uplifted despite the heat, I took time to detour north on the walk back, where, near Mill Run, I found the downy rattlesnake plaintain (*Goodyera pubescens*), a member of the orchid family with an asparagus-like flower stalk, not quite in bloom. As I stepped out to join the main trail, a woodcock flushed and flew across my path, twittering with alarm. Though hearing them sometimes in spring, this was the first I had seen at Soldiers Delight, despite many searches at all hours and seasons. And this at the hottest part of an unlikely summer day. My pagan self would say that this was my reward for returning the "jewel-snake" to its rightful realm.

July *Fierce and Subtle Persistence*

Whorled Milkweed

Fence Lizard

Prairie Warbler

July 1

In summer, the contrast between the lush, humid verdure of the deciduous floodplains and the baking anvils of the serpentine glades and barrens is great. In the middle sector today, the heat and aridity were compounded by recent drought, which has dried up wet spots and left streams the barest trickles. The air was thick with the ever present pitch scent, which in summer mixes with herby smells, insect drones, and dry bird songs to produce a hypnotic, wilting atmosphere among the sun-cracked griddles of rock. The only creatures in a hurry were great spangled fritillaries and neon blue damselflies. All else was heat and lassitude. Lichens and mosses abounded in every shade from emerald to absinthe. Invisible towhees *chewinked,* and the trill of prairie warblers and field sparrows, at long, lazy intervals, only underscored the sense of enervation.

July 5

Cloudy and humid. The commonest moss of the middle sector is easily white cushion moss (*Leucobryum glaucum*), which, as the name implies, resembles a pale, blue-green pincushion, and appears, like some terrestrial sea urchin, in colonies under the gnarled oaks and pines, especially along Chimney Branch. Common also is broom moss (*Dicranum* species), whose light green tufts speckle the ground in the thin oak copses, and cord moss (*Funaria* species), which favors burnt and twig-littered stations where the soil is less acidic. Mosses, or bryophytes, comprise a large and confusing group here. The well-known Smithsonian Institution botanist Clyde F. Reed, who grew up in Baltimore and bicycled to Soldiers Delight as a Depression-era student, has, along with many colleagues, keyed-out at least forty moss varieties in the serpentine alone, including the quite rare *Bryum reedii,* which was named for him.

Above the stream bank itself, joe-pye weed (*Eupatorium* species) is now rising, and greenbriar festoons the pine boughs and cascades into pools. Floating amid these, what looks like spilled petroleum is a natural oil released by decaying plants. Another anomaly visible by the trails and often mistaken for a by-product of human intrusion, is whitened fox scat. It is so common that many mistake it for dog feces, which sometimes dries to a similar paleness. But fox scat is almost always twisted to a hairy point at one end. That foxes are here so numerous, yet largely unseen, is hard for some visitors to grasp.

Climbing the hill beneath the power lines I noticed the lovely color variation in scattered clumps of Indian grass (*Sorghastrum nutans*), ranging from olive to bright green, to bluish and even purple. This is also the dominant grass beside Chimney Branch for much of its course through the serpentine. It will not fruit until late August or September, when the tall stems and feathery seed heads will dress up the glades even further.

Carpeting the ground on many parts of this slope is a low herbaceous plant called dwarf cinquefoil (*Potentilla canadensis*), which resembles, superficially, a kind of wild strawberry. Indeed, it is related to the strawberry, but cinquefoils usually have five compound leaves (thus their name *cinque,* or "five") where strawberries have but three. They are also hardier than strawberries, able to survive thin, porous soils and extremes of heat and dryness. To do this they have evolved root clusters that go down straight and deep, seeking hidden moisture and gripping the soil tightly, so that while their long green-and-red ground runners appear loose and linked to water supplies at the surface, the plant overall is well-secured and safe from drought.

Peter Kalm, the Swedish disciple of the famous taxonomist Carolus Linnaeus, kept fascinating journals of his eclectic discoveries in eastern North America around 1750. He notes that *Potentilla canadensis* was a common remedy for "ague" (influenza) in the region near Philadelphia. It is odd to notice that a bit of botanic nomenclature from that long ago remains unchanged to this day. It jogs one's perspective and allows one to sense the great age of this or any species, closing the wide gap of years in a twinkle of recognition. I will never view dwarf cinquefoil in quite the same way, but look now on the toothed green leaves and prostrate stems as upon some curious antique, imagining dried sprigs littered on an oaken bench, near a hearth-side sickbed in winter, in a world two centuries removed.

July 7

Toward evening I revisited the stone cellar of the old two-story log cabin, and was moved to reflect on the history of white settlement in this place.

When the powerful Susquehannocks had driven the Piscataways south of the Patapsco around 1600, they soon encountered European invaders who surveyed their lands and began to fashion homesteads. A fierce and independent body, who had refused to join the Five (and later Six) Nations of the Iroquois Confederacy further north, the Susquehannocks resisted white encroachment at the same time the Five Nations were punishing them for their waywardness. Seneca warriors were sent south, Piscataways struck north when they could, and new settlers, caught in the middle and soon hating all tribes indiscriminately, became a third formidable opponent. Militia posts were established at Garrison Forest (now Owings Mills) and elsewhere, and patrols and skirmishes became commonplace, as pioneers kept pressure on their foes and began, especially through transmitted diseases, to wear them down.

In less than one hundred years the colonists decimated the Piscataways, drove the Seneca permanently north, and caught the Susquehannocks in a cross fire that bled them to mere dregs. The Susquehannocks, once all-powerful in the region, were reduced to a single peaceful band by 1763, when, during the frontier Indian wars of that year, they sought asylum in the jailyard of Lancaster, Pennsylvania, where they were cornered by a mob and massacred into extinction.

The whites divided their newly captured lands along English lines. The "hundred" of Soldiers Delight Hundred, is an old and imprecise British demarcation, comprising about one hundred "hides" of land. A hide, from the Middle English "hid" (members of a household), meant basically "enough land to support a household," and this ancient measure varied between 80 and 120 acres. Thus a hundred hides might be 8,000 to 12,000 fertile English acres.

But the uncleared lands of America were not crop-fertile at

first, which perhaps accounts for the broad interpretation of hundred as used in such vast tracts as Soldiers Delight Hundred. The "White Grounds" section of that Hundred which included, but was far more extensive than, today's serpentine prairie remnant, was in fact unfarmable. While it and its viable margins were used to graze cattle, it was still an isolated region of shaky productivity. Hardness and poverty persisted there until quite recent times. It provoked frustration, despair, madness. John Berry was not alone in his reactions. A man named Bond axed his wife about 1830, and another named Horn, in 1844, planted his murdered wife in the garden. How many others pondered similar acts, amid the bare poverty and remoteness of old Soldiers Delight?

July 8

Apropos of yesterday's musings, I sought out some of the old mine shafts in Soldiers Delight. Chromite mining here in the nineteenth century was the great industrial success story for a time.

Around 1810, Isaac Tyson, Jr., the son of a wealthy Baltimore merchant, learned from the family gardener, so the story goes, that commercial-grade chromium ore existed on the Tyson estate near what is now Lake Roland. In those days raw ore was shipped to England where it was processed and used to enhance paint pigments. Initial mining and marketing success soon brought Tyson to the mineral outcrops of Soldiers Delight, where in 1817 he began extracting chromite from stream deposits, using sluices to wash and concentrate the granular ore in a way similar to early gold mining. The wooden sluices are more precisely called "buddles," and the streamside mixtures of sand, gravel, and mineral particles fed into them are termed "placer." Chromite grains in placer deposits, like gold, are heavier than the surrounding sand, and will settle out along the floor of the buddle trough when carefully rinsed with water.

Traces of one chromite mining operation are still visible as remnant stone mill-house walls and foundations, fifty feet north of Mill Run, on the road that leads to the fish pond. Chromite ore here was both crushed and buddled, and a series of races and water runs essential to the operation led down from a mill pond upstream. Whether this was part of Tyson's operations, or that of the nearby Harris, and Weir, chrome mines (or possibly all three in successive periods), is unclear.

But it was his discovery, beginning in 1827, of still richer deposits in Harford County and southern Pennsylvania that enabled Tyson to monopolize world chromium production for over twenty years. By the time demand for unprocessed ore began to fall in 1848, he was already extruding valuable chromium compounds himself, with his Baltimore Chrome Works by the Inner Harbor, an enterprise carried into recent times by Allied Chemical Corporation.

A deposit called the Choate Mine became Tyson's chromite mainstay at Soldiers Delight, beginning in 1839. Unlike the surface mining of "chromite sand," this deep-mine technique brought ore up in large chunks, which were then hauled to the streamside mills and buddles for crushing, rinsing, and collecting. The Choate Mine's importance declined by mid-century, but it was still mined on and off for another thirty-five years, and was briefly reopened twice in this century, until the costs of keeping it functionally dry were prohibitive. Today the entrance to this two-hundred-foot-long cavern is easily found just east of Deer Park Road near the overlook.

Besides being a historical curiosity, the Choate Mine exists today as a crude measure of the local water table. In mid-May the main shaft was flooded nearly up to the entrance, and drops of water could be heard plinking eerily in the dark resonant corners. When I stopped by this afternoon, the upper chamber was dry, and though the shaft is distinctly off-limits, a slanting descent of many feet would be needed to reach the new drought-prescribed level.

I contented myself instead looking for long-tailed salamanders (*Eurycea longicauda longicauda*) under rocks by the entrance. This species is fond of mine shafts here, but I have yet to find my first one.

I looped around on what is called the Red Trail, where other small mine pits, either fenced or filled in, edge the pathway. Most likely these were unauthorized diggings, of which there are many at Soldiers Delight. When the price of chromite was high, strapped locals were not above sinking shallow shafts in likely spots, extracting some high-grade ore, and selling it where they could. Especially pure pockets, called "lenses" or "pods," were sometimes found as well, bringing brief cash windfalls to enterprising hunters of chromite.

Meanwhile, placer mining with buddles continued until the 1920s, and was a local cottage industry. The Triplett brothers buddled chromite sand for years at a spot beside Chimney Branch, packing the black grains of ore into half-ton barrels called hogsheads. These were hoisted onto wagons and hauled to Owings Mills, where the railroad took them to Baltimore.

The strength to upend a full hogshead gave a person local celebrity. Several people, including a woman named Black Laura Dorsey, could perform this feat on a regular basis. But overall, buddling for chromite was hard and meager employment, and, by 1928, when the price was but twelve bucks a hogshead, could no longer justify its pursuit.

In the little hollows of the shaft-heads today, I found nothing but lichen-covered serpentinite. Sun beat down on the glades, crickets chirped, and even the prairie warblers had called off singing for the day. I headed back to my car through the heat and pondered the hardness of the "good old days."

July 10

I walked the southeast corner, which is mostly serpentine glades and pine groves. A pair of eastern phoebes were conspicuous, as was a pair of common wood nymph butterflies, mating, back to back in midair.

The morning was clear and bright and breezy, a respite from recent heat and stillness. Cicadas, those background musicians of summer, are now calling steadily. And the big blue jewel of sunny roadsides and waste places, chicory (*Cichorium intybus*), is in full bloom, with its asterlike shape and frayed, square-tipped rays.

Nearby, the honey bee hive in a hollow fallen oak, so active last year, is now abandoned. Most likely the colony fell victim to one of two devastating parasites currently plaguing wild honeybees in the East and elsewhere. Thirty-six states have so far reported infestations of both varroa mites and tracheal mites. The former kill by attaching themselves to the bodies of honeybees, the latter by entering the bees' breathing tubes and choking off their air.

Honeybee varieties somewhat resistent to the mites are now being tested by the USDA, but the short-term prognosis is grim. The mites are capable of destroying most of the wild honeybee population in the U.S., and in Maryland it is estimated that 35 to 50 percent of the honeybees have already been killed.

A great deal is at stake. Unlike bumblebees, wasps, and hornets, honeybees are the only "true pollinators," that is, the only members of the order Hymenoptera that are "flower-true," not flitting from one plant to another to achieve mere random pollination, but returning to the same kind of flower with each flight. Thus, 38 percent of all vegetable matter we consume depends entirely on pollination by honeybees. If it weren't for the wild honeybee, there would not be sufficient food on the planet to support human life at anywhere near its present levels, and unprecedented famine would result.

There is much gypsy moth damage in this part of the park, and a few large trees have died. Woodpeckers, however, seem to profit by this; there are borings and excavations in the bare limbs, and I heard the fussy squeak or cackle of both downy and red-bellied woodpeckers nearby.

Mosses and lichens of subtle hues and textures adorned the outcrops along my return trail, baking in the sunlight or muted in the shade of pines.

July 11

Cloudy and warm. I hiked the middle sector today, from Fraser's driveway out to the power lines, then down to Locust Run.

In a patch of scrubby oaks a warbler sang a song unfamiliar to me: *tootle-tootle-choo-choo-weet-weet.* It was repeated several times before I caught sight of the bird, a male hooded warbler. The bird's usual tune is: *weeta-weeta-weet-see-o!*, or at most a slight variation. This was my first encounter with a member of that species whose voice was so utterly atypical.

Descending the power-line hill to Locust Run I watched both a male scarlet tanager and male red-bellied woodpecker perched ten feet apart on the snags of a dead oak. They seemed to face each other off for a time, changing perches counterclockwise at the same distance apart, and nervously shifting postures.

Summer wildflowers were prominent on this slope: sundrops, chicory, Queen Anne's lace, black-eyed Susan (*Rudbeckia hirta*), and much lavender pink wild bergamot (*Monarda fistulosa*). Near the stream was a tall, striking clump of New York ironweed (*Vernonia noveboracensis*), with its tough maroon stems and violet purple flower clusters. It has bloomed rather early. While pretty, ironweed is a hardy, fast-spreading perennial, and its incursion into the glades presents a threat to rarer, more delicate species, even fameflower, which, in one small location, it has almost shaded out.

Also prominent here were the oddly jointed ears of eastern gamagrass (*Tripsacum dactyloides*), like shiny, hinged knuckles at their bases, thrusting up from five-foot stems.

White-flowered bindweed (*Convolvulus arvensis*) was everywhere by the tiny bridge, entwined like netting in the low bushes. I refreshed myself nearby with many handfuls of ripe wineberries (*Rubus phoenicolasius*), and with a few blackberries as well. The wineberry, sometimes called wine raspberry, is an alien escape introduced from eastern Asia that is now common in Maryland. The fruit is more translucent than that of the cultivated raspberry, and more tart to the taste. It seems to thrive in dry conditions and in partial shade.

Monarch butterflies were about, as were red-spotted purples, alighting on fox dung where the trail reentered the woods.

Hiking back up the power-line hill I came upon an eastern bluebird family—two adults and three recently fledged young—swooping and landing among the steel pylons. And while skirting the fields by the old log cabin I solved the mystery of the broken box turtle shell. A park employee on a tractor was loudly mowing the pasture here. I realized it was just such a machine—perhaps even the same one—that ran over the turtle and crushed its shell. Then a red fox or raccoon ate the flesh.

July 15

Five major streams and their tributaries run through Soldiers Delight: Chimney Branch, Locust Run, Pines Branch, Mill Run, and Red Run. All but the last flow westward to the Patapsco. The true headwaters of three of them lie in various directions beyond the park boundaries. Only Pines Branch and Chimney Branch emanate wholly from within. Pines Branch begins as I described it in my artifact hunts of May, issuing forth at two points from the bottom of a sloping semicircle of farm fields west of Ward's Chapel Road.

This morning I explored the source and initial wanderings of Chimney Branch. Starting from the overlook, I walked down into the middle sector, first left, then right, and found the two headwater branches of this stream, in two nearly parallel gullies. The beds of both were dry. A persimmon (*Dyospyros virginiana*), entwined with poison-ivy (*Rhus radi-*

cans), marks the southern headwater, and a stunted black cherry and black locust (*Robinia pseudo-acacia*) grow beside the northern.

There were many signs of drought. Even the confluence of these branches was dry, and the main stem of Chimney Branch trickled westward at perhaps half its normal flow. Just beyond the power lines and south of this stream is one of Soldiers Delight's most notable natural features. For despite less than an inch of rain in the past two months, this area is wet. In fact it is always wet. It is a kind of grassy delta, initially marked by a bed of spikerush (*Eleocharis* species), where springs and rivulets converge to form odd sinks and meanders. Some have gouged parallel beds only yards apart, while the course of others is hidden amid thick vegetation, pooling in potholes and basins several inches deep. Black-winged damselflies play here, common yellowthroats warble, and fence lizards (*Sceloporus undulatus*) have been seen in the old oaks and pines, sunning themselves on limbs.

The fence lizard is the only lizard to be found at Soldiers Delight. It is perhaps more fond of trees than fences, and is sometimes called pine lizard for its prevalence in dry pine woodlands. Since pine stands are increasing rapidly here, the lizard's numbers here may be growing as well.

One would hardly guess this from casual observation. The creature is difficult to see unless in motion, being a small reptile—seven inches maximum, but usually less—and either dull brown (males) or gray-barred (females) above. Among the gray-brown litter of the glades and piney copses, pinched beneath debris or basking in utter stillness, it keeps a low profile. Fence lizards seem more common or active near Red Dog Lodge, where they are frequently reported and where I saw my first. A young one, just two-inches long, and mimicking—as do all immatures—the herring-bone-on-ash-gray topside of most adult females, it spurted across some leaves like a startled cricket, which is what I first thought it was. Who knows how many youngsters escape notice this way, with their insectlike size and movements?

I continued downstream, stepped along through the boggy spots with care, worked up the main stem, and took my coffee beside a ledge of stratified serpentinite exposed by centuries of flow. It was that rare summer day when heat and humidity are low, and skies are clear blue and breezy. The damselflies turned in the light and shadow, changing from neon green to blue and just as quickly back, wrens and chickadees chattered, and, up on the hillsides, breezes rustled the leather-leaved oaks with a sound that brought back my youth.

July 17

Hot. The cicadas are droning fiercely. In the middle sector, at the boggy delta beside Chimney Branch, the springs continue to send forth fresh trickles that collect in nearby pools. These open pools float with rainbows of natural oil and reddish iron oxide. Bright green bubbles form atop the gummy submerged tresses of common water moss (*Fontinalis* species). Conspicuous again are black-winged damselflies, though these are mostly females, which, with their dark non-metallic body tones and white wing patches, or "stigma," look like a different species entirely.

At least three spikerush varieties appear in this wet place. They are members of the sedge family (*Cyperaceae*) and, while resembling grasses, differ from them in having solid, jointless stems, multiple edges, and a leaf sheath that joins tightly, not openly, to the stem. Those here are bright yellow-green, six inches to two feet tall, with seeds clustered on terminal spikes.

When one presses down on the silty ground-surface here, air and gases erupt from below in rapid bubbles. Whirligig beetles and other *Gyrinidae* sport in the shallow pools, whose bottoms are dark with decayed vegetation. Young red maples edging the water have numerous leaf galls, which appear like tiny "pimples" in shades from green to black.

Further downstream I came upon isolated clumps of a bright green moss that clung to wet rocks at bankside. One peninsula of purplish serpentinite had vivid chartreuse pads of it growing from its base. Here I captured a lovely moth that rested on this moss and resembled a pinkish sunflower seed.

At a bend I surprised a green-backed heron who'd been dining on the dozens of dace that were massed in the largest pool. Moss-pink grows with the mosses here, in prickly, lime green carpets. Nearby, too, I found knee-high specimens of rose-pink (*Sabatia angularis*), a member of the gentian family, which has just begun to bloom. This year it is sparsely scattered, but in some summers it is numerous in the glades and broader prairies, apparently subject to population explosions under favorable conditions. A second bend intruded and ridges hemmed me in, creating a sense of seclusion heightened by the half-echo of water purling loudly over ledges. I sat upon a mossy rock and listened only to the stream.

July 20

Heat and humidity have made explorations unpleasant. At home I identified that moth of the 17th as a painted lichen moth (*Hypoprepia fucosa*). Lichens are its only food.

A further note on local history: The origin of the name Soldiers Delight is a subject of conjecture. Since the name, as part of "Soldiers Delight Hundred," appears in records as early as the 1600s, I do not buy the popular theory that it is a corruption of "Sollers," a common local surname. If the place was a "Hundred" in the seventeenth century, that is, a vast roughly surveyed district belonging to no one family, then it would not have been named for a Soller, or anyone else.

Nor do I accept the sentimental favorite: that patrolling soldiers were treated to pastry or ice-cream "delights" by local ladies. Local ladies of that time were dirt-poor drudges who, should they once have had the price of sugar, were unlikely, or unable, to lavish the commodity on companies of militia.

And the theory that Soldiers Delight was a hunter's paradise and thus was the "delight" of those same armed and hungry patrols, does not consider that adjacent regions were at least as game-rich.

Another idea, that its trailless tangles and dense foliage "delighted" the rangers by concealing them from Indians is ludicrous. The Indians were past-masters at the ways of concealment and would hardly have been much disadvantaged by foliage conditions, conditions that, considering the nature of serpentine soil, were more likely to have been revealing than concealing.

The word delight was a term applied—often half-facetiously—to many early land holdings. In fact, an old map of the area lists both Bank's Delight and Molly and Sally's Delight, as well as Brown's Chance, Lewe's Fancy, Well's Prospect, Maile's Adventure, and Chavy's Chase. The word delight expressed pleasure with the privilege of grant or ownership, hope for the future, and ironic determination in the face of appalling frontier hardship. In this case—the region early on being little used except by transient militia—Soldiers Delight was a simple and ironic description of its original utility, with delight wryly connoting ownership—i.e., constant troop presence—after the verbal fashion of the time. That's my theory, anyway.

The late local historian, Edward Spencer, in part backs this up, suggesting that the old Baltimore County Rangers, forever plagued by the region's hardships, christened it Soldiers Delight in a tongue-in-cheek spirit of irony, just as one of the roughest roads in the area was named Featherbed Lane.

July 23

I spent a morning in the glades on the hottest day of the decade. In the middle sector, just after seven, there was still dew on the grass beside Chimney Branch, and a smell of dampness and pines. Crickets were chirping, and the first cicada kicked in, loudly, at about eight o'clock. Each bird present contributed the barest song or call, starting with field sparrows, rufous-sided towhees, and white-eyed vireos, then Carolina chickadees, tufted titmice, gray catbirds, American crows, and downy woodpeckers. By nine o'clock I had also heard American goldfinch, blue-gray gnatcatcher, northern cardinal, Acadian flycatcher, red-bellied woodpecker, and prairie warbler. This is a good sample of gladeside breeding birds, with perhaps common yellowthroat, hooded warbler, yellow-breasted chat, and indigo bunting conspicuously absent.

The dace, both rosyside (*Clinostomus funduloides*) and blacknose (*Rhinichthys atratulus*), are now tightly corralled in the remnant pools of the streambed, and panic easily, writhing and flashing their rainbow or steel flanks at one's near approach.

The streambed itself is reddish brown serpentinite, full of iron oxide, with occasional facets of orange or yellow, formed long ago by hardened solutions of bright granular pigments.

A few leaves of red maple have already gone half pink from drought and spilled their accent in the stream. And spotted wintergreen (*Chimaphila maculata*), which I've found in both the deciduous woods and dry pine groves, I now discovered in a grassy brookside glade. Its close relative, pipsissewa (*Chimaphila umbellata*), can be found toward Red Dog Lodge. Nearby, too, was rose-pink, large-flowered partridge-pea (*Cassia fasciculata*), the low-growing green milkweed (*Asclepias viridiflora*), and whorled milkweed (*Asclepias verticillata*).

Whorled milkweed, not to be confused with a smaller serpentine inhabitant, whorled milkwort (*Polygala verticillata*), is on the DNR's Watchlist for threatened state species, and is one of the oddest plants in the area. Here it seems to prefer the glade edges, partly shaded by scrubby trees. Looking like no other milkweed I've ever seen, it bears as much resemblance to common milkweed as a pine does to an oak. Its leaves are linear, that is, straight and thin, much like those of conifers. Linear leaves are another common plant adaptation to living in serpentine soil. Their needle thinness resists scorching and excessive heat, their toughness retains moisture and baffles insects, and they require less energy to produce.

In fact, it is such a popular adaptation that whorled milkweed eluded me when I first began to seek it. Both young blazing-star (*Liatris* species) and new shoots of pines are linear-leaved, and somewhat resemble this milkweed, while competing in the same terrain. Whorled milkweed at Soldiers Delight blooms modestly in late summer, but until then is inconspicuous, looking like a fresh little conifer.

Some individuals here don't bloom at all. Both the serpentine soil and too much shade seem to retard them, as they do other species, so finding a textbook specimen, with its crown of tiny flowers and eventual slender seedpods, is difficult in some years. I don't recommend it, but for sure identification one can simply break a leaf or stem, when a milky juice should then bead faintly at the fracture. The erect pods, or follicles, are unmistakable. Frequently just one per plant, they are shaped like some species of aquatic leech, or like slim jalapeño peppers: elongate affairs, finger-length and bear-claw thin, and packed, like those of their commoner cousins, with the silky, down-tipped seeds so dispersive in the slightest breeze. Whorled milkweed is altogether an outrageous plant here, sulking in the shadows, defying its common name, inwardly hiding the secrets of its kind, even sometimes giving you the finger of its sole erectile fruit.

The reported high temperature at Westminster today was 105 degrees.

July 25

Mercifully cloudy. I explored the lake coves of Locust Run and Pines Branch. It was a shock to see how low the water has dropped—at least five full feet—after its springtime high.

Lest anyone doubt the predatory fierceness of largemouth bass, I observed a three-inch fingerling of that species chasing minnows of nearly the same length. In a shallow pool it drove a whole school before it in panic, like some watery wolf.

Groups of tiger swallowtails (*Papilio glaucus*), which first appeared in April, now feed on the exposed mud of the cove, in groups of five or more. Concentrated minerals are the attraction. Meanwhile, a milky blue scum of algae coats the remnant pools nearby.

Only the main channel of Locust Run, perhaps five yards wide and cut deeply into the lake bed, still holds any quantity of water. The beaver have chewed the once-submerged tree stumps into pointed stakes, and I examined the subtle entrance to a bankside lodge which now sits high and dry. A second lodge was started beside the main channel, but has also been left exposed. The channel—the same one I floated my line in last April—still flows with a languid current. Goldfinches flit now from snags and stumps that were recently well under water.

Further on I watched huge carp (*Cyprinus carpio*) patrol the margins of the shrunken cove, sifting the silt, tails up, tan bodies tilting. When startled they dart away, leaving cloudy wakes. In one fifty foot stretch of shoreline I counted thirty-four carp, one to two feet long, and others could be seen further out.

Tracks were everywhere in the surrounding mud: red fox, raccoon, and white-tailed deer prints, and the large, three-pronged impressions left by patient great blue herons.

In a little bay up toward Pines Branch were visible, on the bottom in six inches of water, the remnant spring spawning beds of bass: circles a foot in diameter, fanned out by the male and edged by the pebbles thus expelled.

Among quartzite outcrops along the shoreline I found several crude "fish-tail" spear-point pre-forms, and a few flakes and fractures. A young smallmouth bass (*Micropterus dolomieui*) cruised the green-tinted shallows below one of the rock piles I was searching.

It is the busy season for many spiders, especially those little orb-weavers, the *Micrathena*. They string their webs across trails and tracks, and drag themselves, oversized abdomens and all, to safety when travelers crash through their handiwork. Shortcutting back through the woodlands, I swept a stick before me to keep from being constantly clotheslined.

July 27

Donna and I walked this morning on the fire lanes beside Liberty Lake. The deep summer shade in the woodlands was torn throughout with jagged pools of sunlight. Square-stemmed monkey-flower (*Mimulus ringens*) hung its blue heads at trailside, and yellow-billed cuckoos called with languid monotony.

Many young birds, recently fledged, are about, voicing inept renditions of their proper calls, an activity confusing to birders.

The Japanese beetles (*Popillia japonica*) are thick this year. Blackberry in particular has been ravaged by them, leaving low hedges of lacey leaf skeletons.

I captured two green tiger beetles (*Cinindela* species) on the roadbed, where they often hunt. Normally fast and elusive, they were sluggish, perhaps due to last night's shower.

These are the bright, metallic green insects often seen by forest hikers.

Some black walnut trees (*Juglans nigra*) have already fruited, and the nuts of hickory (*Carya* species)—both the big four-ribbed husks of shagbark (*C. ovata*) and mockernut (*C. tomentosa*), and the small-husked bitternuts (*C. cordiformis*)—are dropping beside the trails.

July 30

I walked the eastern sector on a warm sunny morning, after several damp days. The berries of tall, purple-stemmed pokeweed (*Phytolacca americana*) are ripening, and a black tupelo (*Nyssa sylvatica*) has colored early, its leaves already half scarlet.

Orchard grass (*Dactylis glomerata*) has fruited in the wetter parts of the trail, the brown seed heads drooping with scarecrow limpness. Ferns are conspicuous, especially hay-scented fern (*Dennstaedtia punctilobula*), which covers whole hillsides in this sector and exudes a faint odor of new-mown hay. Near Red Run, Christmas fern (*Polystichum acrostichoides*), an evergreen variety, is common, especially in the damp floodplain.

A fixture of the late summer glades, blazing-star, with its purplish, thistlelike spires, is starting to bloom by the dry trail margins, some plants stretching two feet tall. While officially listed as grass-leaved blazing-star (*Liatris graminifolia*), there is evidence to suggest that most of the Soldiers Delight plants are dense blazing-star (*Liatris spicata*), as the flowerheads are "sessile," that is, attached directly to the main stem. *Liatris spicata* is highly rare in Maryland. Smartweed (*Polygonum* species), of several varieties, crowds the path elsewhere, and naked flowered tick-trefoil (*Desmodium nudiflorum*) presents tiny violet blossoms on long leafless spikes.

Three tree species with similar toothy leaves, American chestnut (*Castanea dentata*), chestnut oak (*Quercus prinus*), and Allegheny chinkapin (*Castanea pumila*), can be found here. American chestnut was all but wiped out in this century by a foreign fungus, but continues to generate from stumps in the East, usually dying before maturity. One specimen, which was bowed across the path here, would, if straightened, have stood over twenty feet tall.

While sipping coffee above Red Run, I had one of those wildlife encounters so common to aimless wandering. Within a five minute span I was visited by a curious redstart, a Kentucky warbler, and a young hooded warbler, the latter approaching to four feet as I sat very still on the ground. Is there something attractive to birds about harmless and indolent humans? Perhaps their extreme rarity.

When I rose to continue, my second summer encounter with woodcocks occurred: first one, then another, came bursting up through the laurel by the creek, twittering and whirring as they fled.

The state-rare fameflower, which I first observed in June, is surprisingly common in some of the glades. Just west of the floodplain here, on a serpentine ridge, is a scattered colony. Its pink flowers contrast nicely with its pale, frost green bases, and it clings here and there in the stoney soil, often ringed by sprays of chickweed. For those seeking it there is first surprise with this relative abundance, then wonder at the deftness of its secrecy. The lingering sense it leaves, though, as one scans the rocky hills and sweats in the glaring sun, is of fierce and subtle persistence, and of the deep fragility of life.

August *The Sweetest Nuts in Nature*

Tiger Swallowtail

Blazing-Star

Yellow-billed Cuckoo

August 2

The late summer palette of the prairie glades is beginning to be loaded with color. I briefly walked the middle sector along Chimney Branch this morning. Purple ironweed, deep lavender blazing-star, blushing rose-pink, bright ocher partridge pea, white Queen Anne's lace, and chrome yellow gray goldenrod (*Solidago nemoralis*)—the flowers of all these plants are mixing their pigments among the grasses and viney tangles.

More subtle is the joe-pye weed (*Eupatorium* species), now on the verge of blooming. This is the pale reddish, flat-crowned flower so common to weedy habitats and attractive to many butterflies. Though, like Queen Anne's lace, a European alien, it has been around so long that it draws a pleasant spark of recognition from even the oldest hikers and gardeners.

Another weedy but far smaller plant to be found by this stream is tick-trefoil. Showing frail pinkish blossoms on slender stalks, the species here at first seemed to me a cross between small-leaved tick-trefoil (*Desmodium ciliare*) and large-bracted tick-trefoil (*D. cuspidatum*), its leaf habit not quite fitting either variety as described by the field guides. But this, I learned, is linear-leaved tick-trefoil (*Desmodium lineatum*), a species, along with rigid tick-trefoil (*Desmodium rigidum*), indigenous to serpentine and now rare in Maryland.

A major difficulty for plants growing in serpentine soils is poor nutrition. High levels of magnesium and other minerals inhibit the uptake of nutrients, particularly calcium. Thus certain plants at Soldiers Delight have become ultra-efficient at absorbing calcium, while others, like members of the legume or pea family—to which the tick-trefoils belong— probably manage to survive here by producing some nutrients themselves. The roots of Leguminosae have developed a symbiotic relationship with specialized bacteria that allows them to capture the important nutrient, nitrogen, even when it is absent from the soil. These bacteria live in small bulges, or "nodules," on the roots of the legumes, and are able to trap atmospheric nitrogen, "fix" it in the soil (that is, hold and reprocess it), and thus allow the plant roots to absorb it in their usual way, as though the soil were nitrogen-fertile to begin with.

Perhaps this explains the large number of legume species at Soldiers Delight. In the serpentine soils below the power-cut I have found, besides the rare rigid and linear-leaved tick-trefoils, several more common tick-trefoil species, as well as the *Lespedezas*—low, cloverlike legumes with trailing stems— and the hairy little legume *Crotalaria sagittalis,* or rattlebox, which forms leathery pods in August that clatter like wee maracas.

August 4

Today I caught a tiger swallowtail butterfly with my bare hands. I gently pinched its wings between my fingers as it sat on a wet spot by the stream. Then I let it go.

When I was a child I never caught the tiger swallowtail, even with a net, for they were rare in my city neighborhood, and moved through swiftly when they came. In those days they amazed me greatly, and I thought them magic creatures. It seemed natural that I could not capture them.

Now, though still beautiful, they amaze me less, and I catch them with ease.

To some extent, nature relieves acquisitiveness. It makes one aware, by its sheer multiplicity and scope, that it is, in any material sense, beyond possession and ownership. Of course, people can, and do, collect tokens of its beauty: butterflies, beetles, flowers, shells—bright little shards of its physical bulk, fragments of its awesome fecundity.

Yet far from quenching desire, these may become mocking symbols of how paltry is our grasp, how petty all such striving. The power of nature's beauty lies in passage, in its wan evanescence, in the unswerving imperative of the fragile and fleeting, and in the certainty of wilt. The details of this beauty are in one sense microcosmic, cellular distillations of some human longing beyond fulfillment, condensed briefly in the crenulations on the hind wing of a butterfly.

But in the end, one must not clutch merely at hind wings, or the precise metric length of lobes and crenulations. One must clutch at a larger prize. Let the whole show thrash before you, let it creep and glimmer and wink, and, when you finally settle down, drop your tiny net, and lean back on your idle hands beneath some uncollected sky, in some unreduced landscape, the prize just might drop in your lap.

August 7

I went up north of Ward's Chapel Road, in the eastern end of the northwest sector. The feeder branches of Mill Run are bone dry, not even trickling as they did last month. Moss-phlox leaves spread their prickly green rugs along the edges of the glades, and grooved yellow flax (*Linum sulcatum*), a regionally rare species, is blooming here and there among the serpentinite outcrops.

The healthy colony of fameflower in the rocky depression, which I found blooming in early June, is being crowded by New York ironweed, a far more showy but utterly common flower.

I rested near the mouth of a small cave or pit, hoping to glimpse a fence lizard. Instead a young deer, with fawn spots still visible, emerged from the edge of a pine grove to watch me from fifty yards off.

Another mine pit near here, largely filled in, offers a sloping tunnel descent, body width, to the cooler depths below. I probed the entrance on all fours, hoping for long-tailed salamanders, but had no success.

August 8

I walked the northwest sector on a cloudy afternoon. Masses of blue chicory and white Queen Anne's lace enliven the farm-field trails. The flowers of horse nettle (*Solanum carolinense*), a prickly pasture "weed," are surprisingly lovely: star-shaped, and with alternate shades of dark and pale lavender among petals on the same stem.

The fruits of wild black cherry are now ripe and profuse on several trees beside the woods. Dark cherries a half-inch thick hang in long pendulate clusters, dozens to a stem.

In the woods above Mill Run grows hay-scented fern, Christmas fern, sensitive fern (*Onoclea sensibilis*), and a fourth round-lobed species I cannot name.

I paused in a ravine here simply to look and listen. Now and then I must force myself to stop "reducing" nature through identification, and instead take in the whole. A portion of every outing is reserved for this.

But soon the need to find and name takes over again, in this year of studied exploration. I noted that there is much common spicebush (*Lindera benzoin*), maple-leaf viburnum (*Viburnum acerifolium*), and jack-in-the-pulpit in this section of woods, the latter having just set its fruit, a tight cluster of bright red berries on the erect stem of the spadix, a foot or so off the ground.

Acorns, varying from flat to full-bodied, are already falling from the large northern red oaks (*Quercus rubra*) along the Mill Run trail. Further on, false Solomon's-seal (*Smilacina* species) tangles the lush floodplain. And just as hay-scented fern is the commonest fern species above Red Run, here it is the evergreen Christmas fern.

August 11

Donna and I meandered in the eastern sector this morning. The blazing-star is now positively *blazing* along the glade trails, its magenta purple spikes knee-high and as fuzzy as thistle. Like all the *Liatris* it has long tap roots, sometimes fifteen feet deep, while in spring the bulbous roots have a carrotlike flavor and were sometimes eaten by Indians. The deep root system helps it survive in the dry serpentine soils. Pure white flower forms of this *Liatris* occur commonly in the glades as do shades of the palest lavender.

Exploring off the trail at one point, we both cursed the barriers of thorny vines. The botanical integrity of the prairie fragments continues to be threatened not only by the incursion of pines and cedars, but by rampant herbaceous plants, foremost among the latter being common greenbriar. This hardy green vine, sometimes called catbriar because of its clawlike thorns, has enveloped large sections of Soldiers Delight, not only blotting out prairie glades, but sealing off human access. For such oath-provoking behavior it has gained the nicknames "tramps' troubles" and "blasphemy-vine." It is beginning to set its grapelike fruits now, which at least provide food for songbirds and other creatures.

Multiflora rose (*Rosa multiflora*) is almost as pernicious. Once promoted by agriculturists for erosion control and animal cover, it grows and proliferates wildly, defies eradication, and sports fearsome needle-sharp thorns—some a full inch long—on climbing whiplike branches. At Soldiers Delight it sometimes mingles with common greenbriar to form daunting, smothering walls. But it, too, has a plus side, and the hips will be ripe red browse for wildlife through the winter and early spring.

August 14

If there is anything quieter than a wood warbler working south in fall migration, then I don't know what it is. Some are present now—though it is not technically autumn—migrating down through the forests and groves and receiving little notice.

At another wild location a bird-bander friend of mine kept mist nets—from August through October—in a power line cut between two woodlots, for a number of years. On a given morning at this time of year one could walk the power-cut, ears tuned and binoculars at ready, for half an hour, and find nothing but the odd catbird or goldfinch. Yet a look at the nets every twenty minutes revealed trapped warblers and other migrants in surprising variety and plenty. At a table nearby, in the course of a season, were banded mourning, Connecticut, golden-winged, cerulean, prothonotary, even orange-crowned warblers, as well as all the commoner species—enough to excite the envy of any East Coast birder. But you'd have never guessed their presence from a simple walk through the area.

Many birds, especially warblers, "skulk" their way through autumn migration. Competitive singing has ceased, weather is often mild, foliage is lush. Broken flocks and family groups disperse wearily through the trees or undergrowth, purged of breeding urgency and conserving vital strength. Many are young birds, shy, drab, and inept, still learning the ways of forage and peregrination. None are conspicuous.

Thus it didn't surprise me when I saw not a single warbler on a two hour walk this morning, in all the best habitat. They are around, I know, in varying numbers, but setting the tone of tired quiet that is the harbinger of fall.

August 15

This morning I decided to check the water quality along Chimney Branch. One way of doing this is to lift small rocks in the streambed and look for insect nymphs and larvae (among other differences, nymphs do not undergo a pupal, or resting, stage before adulthood; larvae do). Rocks about six inches wide are best. The healthiest streams will contain the nymphs of mayflies (order Ephemeroptera) and stoneflies (order Plecoptera), and the larvae of caddisflies (order Trichoptera).

In one small stretch of Chimney Branch I found many nymphs of both mayflies and stoneflies. The one northern caddisfly (family *Limnephilidae*) larva I found was typically disguised in a case it had built of leaf-bits and sand.

Quite common were dragonfly nymphs (order *Odonata*), nearly an inch long. These are voracious predators, and when I made the mistake of leaving one in the same container with both a mayfly and stonefly nymph, I returned to find it had devoured its fellow captives.

Beneath a midstream log I found a queen snake (*Natrix septemvittata*), about a foot long but, unfortunately, dead. This species feeds almost exclusively on crayfish, and is a well-documented, but secretive, resident of Soldiers Delight.

A small sedge appears near this location, but with variable abundance. Annual fimbry (*Fimbristylis annua*) is at home in the desert Southwest, but also shows up on the serpentine outcrops of the East. Seeds may live in the soil for years, quite undetected, until a sudden surplus of rain allows them to shoot up and flower.

August 17

Today I went fishing. I took a rod and reel, some hooks and bobbers and worms, and walked up to the fish pond in the northwest sector of Soldiers Delight.

I sat on the bank by some common cattails (*Typha latifolia*), until before long something dragged my bobber under, and I reeled in a tiny fish. This was a bluegill (*Lepomis macrochirus*), a colorful member of the sunfish family with a blue-black patch on its gill cover. These fish are widely stocked, often in combination with largemouth bass. Sure enough, not long after releasing the bluegill I caught a miniature largemouth bass; at six inches in length it was hardly more than a fingerling.

The old Stivers house, not quite visible through the pines above the pond (and currently being rented), is the reason for both the pond and its fish. Long ago the owners scraped out a hole in the fields, dammed a branch of Mill Run, and stocked the resulting reservoir. Since then they've moved away, the woods have grown up by the banks, and the pond has silted in. In fact it has silted in so badly that the water is but a few feet deep. The fish are crowded and stunted, and harassed by assorted predators. Once my bobber went under and I reeled a big snapping turtle half way to shore before it thrashed its escape. Snappers gobble up pond fish like picnickers gobble grapes. With little room to maneuver certain fish can be greatly depleted.

I caught a few more bluegills and enjoyed my little junket, but the pond's future is not in fish or fishing. The cattails will encroach, the silt will collect, the pond will become a small marsh, and then a part of the woodland. Meanwhile, it's a good habitat for herons, for ducks and frogs and swallows. And especially for hungry turtles.

August 22

That dominant grass of the prairie glades, little bluestem, is now becoming conspicuous. The prettiest examples of this species alternate segments of bluegreen and glaucous magenta, taking turns at each stem joint.

Indeed most of the grass species have matured along the trails, especially the colorful Indian grass, with its clumps of slender sword-blade leaves shaded anywhere from green to purple, and its plumelike panicles mixed with orange gold, chartreuse, and maroon.

A few grasses, such as the fescues (*Festuca* species), have already matured, dispersed their seeds, and dried to a buffy straw. Some grasses even bloomed last spring, like the rare and celebrated holy grass (*Hierochloe odorata*), also called sweetgrass, vanilla grass, or Seneca grass. The Indians used this fragrant grass to make baskets, while in Europe it was scattered by the doors of churches, to perfume the way at Easter and other vernal holidays. It grows beside bogs and wet places, and most manuals list it as occurring no further south than New Jersey. Yet long ago the late Maryland botanist George Russell Fessenden discovered it in small amounts at Soldiers Delight.

Perhaps its biggest appreciator at the park, however, was the biologist and agristologist Elmer Worthley, whose death this past June ended his long love affair with Soldiers Delight. Fiercely attached to the natural world, he himself was credited with discovering a Peruvian moss, and a lichen-eating beetle found in Florida by one of his students, was named for Elmer. The surprise of both holy grass, and tufted hairgrass (*Deschampsia caespitosa*), another lover of wet places that is unexpected in Maryland, delighted Elmer Worthley, and he tried to educate others about the wonder of these and other rare Soldiers Delight flora.

Elmer's efforts were equaled, if not exceeded, by those of his wife, Jean Worthley. Where Elmer was gruff, Jean is the soul of kindness and cheerful erudition. A lifelong area resi-

dent, expert on local plants—especially at Soldiers Delight—
and former hostess of the popular children's television show
"Hodge Podge Lodge," Jean continues to sensitize children
and adults alike to subtle natural glories. She knows the great
secret of education, which is to praise and encourage. Make
two stupid comments out of three, and she will focus on your
one bright remark, and lift you and make you shine. She sees
the child—and therefore the vulnerable lover and seeker—in
all who approach nature, and by loving this in each, finds her
love returned manyfold.

August 24

One of Elmer Worthley's pet peeves was the botanical confusion created by numerous and imprecise common names.
He therefore became obstinate to a fault about using only
Latin. I can't entirely sympathize. The real fun of natural discovery—its beauty, surprise, mystery, and whimsy—is re-
flected, however briefly, in the poetry of common names. Ap-
preciation and inspiration, not system, are the sweetest nuts
in nature. Linnaeun classification is a cog in the machine of
understanding, not understanding itself.

Still, I can see his point of view. Merely among the best-
known eastern wildflowers there are thirteen hundred species
in eighty-four families, and that doesn't include trees and
shrubs, or grasses, sedges, and rushes. Then consider that
many have multiple common names, and you've got some
real potential problems.

A case in point occurred this morning. Someone at the
overlook asked me where to find broomsage. I couldn't give
him a simple answer. It is also called broomsedge, but is nei-

ther a sage nor a sedge. In fact it is another grass of the genus *Andropogon,* of which my grasses manual lists 263 species and subspecies. The common name for all the *Andropogon* is beardgrass, which means that, in common name terms, someone looking for broomsage or broomsedge is also looking for beardgrass.

To further confuse things, two of the best-known beardgrasses at Soldiers Delight are little bluestem and big bluestem (*Andropogon gerardi*). So broomsage or broomsedge is not only a beardgrass, but beardgrass is a bluestem. None, however, are to be confused with bristlegrass (*Setaria* species), which also grows here and is of several varieties.

The man may have wanted little or big bluestem, which are, of course, easy to find at Soldiers Delight. But *Andropogon virginicus,* a Southern species used commonly in the past to fashion broom heads, is the one most specific to the common name broomsedge. Or broomsage. I think!

August 27

Cloudy, warm, and humid. Amid the lush monotony of late summer foliage the blazing-star, now at peak bloom, adds welcome color in the eastern sector, especially along the trails near the glades.

The park's breeding bird species, of which I now list eighty-one, are silent, and a few have already departed. Mostly there is the wan "cricket quiet" of approaching autumn, broken here and there with a blue jay screech or goldfinch twitter, amplified by the stillness.

As soon as one approaches even the driest creek, that lover of damp ground, ironweed, shows its striking purple bloom.

On my way back through the pines west of Red Run, a bird bolted past in zigzag flight, neatly dodging trees. Thinking it one of the agile *Accipiter* hawks, I was surprised to see, when it landed, a shy looking yellow-billed cuckoo. It, or another of its species, was the last thing I heard when I reached my car: a measured, far away rhythm, *chook ... chook ... chook,* just audible through the trees.

August 30

Before it got too hot this morning, I headed back along Red Run, to the place where the eagle landed. Two years ago this fall, a golden eagle perched in a dead tree here—had probably roosted overnight in migration—and I had managed to see it.

What interests me now is the roost tree. An old chestnut oak, perhaps killed by gypsy moths, it collapsed last winter in a storm and is serving its final purpose.

The first thing I found were the beak holes from three sizes of woodpeckers: small downies, mid-size red-bellieds, and jumbo pileateds. They had flaked off bark in their labors, leaving sections of pith exposed. On the pith, beneath large pieces of bark, on various limbs and branches, and under the trunk where it touched the ground, I found the following forms of life: four varieties of mosses and four of lichens, thirteen varieties of fungi (including four "bracket" types), six species of spiders, three species of millipedes, seven species of adult flying insects (both active and inactive), the larvae of six insect species, two species of sow bugs, two of earthworms, a crayfish, a garden slug, and a red-backed sala-mander. A number of plants, especially ferns, grew nearby, birds scolded my intrusion, and there was evidence of small mammals.

The oak had seen life as a deer-browsed sapling, as a mature tree housing animals, sloughing oxygen and moisture, and enriching the soil, and as an aging giant releasing its vigor to parasites. But once dead—erect or fallen—the oak's utility never ceased. Indeed, in some sense, in this last stage of existence it was most supportive of life.

September *The Old-Gold Light of Autumn*

Serpentine Aster

Sandplain Gerardia

Leopard Frog

September 1

The first day of September arrived like the first day of autumn: with a Canadian cold front, recalling the clear, crisp air and brilliant skies of the upper Midwest.

The several varieties of gerardia (*Agalinis*) found at Soldiers Delight are now in full bloom. These showy members of the figwort family are distinguished primarily by small differences in flower construction, and, to a lesser extent, by foliage and habitat. The big, bell-like blossoms of purple gerardia (*A. purpurea*), deep pink to rose purple in hue, are hardest to confuse with their relatives in the area, holding exclusively to the moist serpentine streamsides, and sporting inch-deep corollas. However, sandplain gerardia (*A. acuta*), as well as slender gerardia (*A. tenuifolia*)—both with smaller flowers— share similar habitats among the drier slopes and glades, and sometimes require a hand lens to sort out. *A. acuta* is a globally rare species; its most healthy and extensive population anywhere on the planet—about 90 percent of all the plants in existence—occurs at Soldiers Delight.

No one really knows for certain how many species of *Agalinis* now survive here. It is something of a mystery, perhaps never to be solved. Most members of this lovely genus are annuals, and the seeds they disperse are of variable dormancy, sometimes lying fallow for one, two, three, even five or more years before conditions are right for germination. In addition, the genus is often parasitic, actually "hemi-parasitic," that is, parasitic on only *half* of certain other plants. In the case of *Agalinis,* that half is the root system, usually of trees such as oak or grasses like little bluestem.

So the plant's life cycle is complex: in many cases, species of *Agalinis* must first set and disperse seeds successfully, then the seeds must find proper conditions for germination within their highly variable span of viability, and finally the germinated seedlings may need an appropriate nearby root system to parasitize (survival is not wholly dependent on this parasitization, but is enhanced by it).

The problem for the botanical surveyor and indexer at Soldiers Delight is one of logistics and timing. Amid some twelve hundred acres of appropriate habitat, he or she must try to locate various species of the genus—verifiable only by their flower structure—in minute and widely scattered theoretical locations, somehow coinciding the search with unpredictable germination years, and all during the eight- to ten-week season of the plant's blooming. A daunting task indeed!

Currently, besides the aforementioned species, records at Soldiers Delight exist for *A. obtusifolia* (also classified, in the Piedmont, as *A. decemloba*), although it has not been found —but not systematically searched for, either—since 1967. It also seems likely that *A. fasciculata,* another lover of dry places, exists at Soldiers Delight (though no specimen has been confirmed since 1973). So the present inventory includes at least three extant species and perhaps as many as five. Who knows? There may be more; at least two other dry-ground species exist in Maryland. To uncover the true number here, it would probably take a botanical search far more intensive than is good for the current fragile habitat.

This morning the purple gerardia was particularly attractive beside the stream path in the middle sector, mixing with the yellow of partridge pea and the dark violet of ironweed. A broad touch of white was added by white snakeroot (*Eupatorium rugosum*) and boneset (*Eupatorium perfoliatum*), displaying their new flat-topped clusters amid the lush floodplain tangles.

September 3

Clear, cool, and dry. It is the season of mature grasses. I walked beside Chimney Branch in the middle sector this morning, and right away a white-eyed vireo called loudly: *Chip!-wheep-chuck-a-luck!* Another male of the species sounded from across the hillside, while all else—save for the low squeak of crickets—was silence.

The stalks of little bluestem in the glades continue to evolve with varied color, principally bluegreen, turquoise, and glaucous magenta. Much of the joe-pye weed bloom, meanwhile, is already beginning to fade.

Among butterflies, pearly crescents (*Phyciodes tharus*) and silver-spotted skippers (*Epargyreus clarus*) are now common. Monarchs balance drunkenly on the milkweeds, and the lovely buckeye (*Junonia coenia*)—fondly remembered from the alleys of my childhood—alights on clumps of boneset. Similarly, blue jays, calling near and far amid the pre-autumnal quiet, convey a nostalgic poignancy.

The two ubiquitous "yellows" of the season, goldenrods and goldfinches, enliven the sloping hillsides. Here, too, green foxtail, or bristlegrass (*Setaria viridis*), has ripened, as has purpletop (*Tridens flavus*). I noticed that a little grove of quaking aspen—several dozen saplings only three or four feet high—have taken hold on the power-cut slope. Meanwhile, slender knotweed (*Polygonum tenue*), a humble, spike-branched member of the buckwheat family that blotches the autumn glades in low green bunches, is setting its knotlike buds in the axes of its linear leaves.

On my way back, beside the road from Red Dog Lodge, I found a single ripe specimen of poverty-grass (*Aristida dichotoma*), one of the two species of three-awn found here, and easily the most common. The three-awns are named for the delicate trio of needle-thin awns, or flexible bristles, attached to each flowering scale. When the scales mature to seeds, awns—usually single or double on other grasses—serve to catch the wind, or the coats of passing animals, enhancing dispersal.

And just below the overlook were a few foot-high specimens of that dry-country orchid, the slender ladies' tresses (*Spirathes gracilis*), with their spiral pinnacles of tiny white flowers.

September 4

Cloudy and a bit cool. One of the least appreciated rare species of Soldiers Delight is the serpentine aster (*Aster depauperatus*). Appearing singly or in bunches among the outcrops, this humble species has tiny composite flowers resembling those of the common small white aster (*Aster vimineus*), yet it evolved only on serpentine soils, occurs at but four locations in Maryland, and is a candidate for federal protection.

The leaves are the most obviously distinctive feature of *A. depauperatus*. They are linear, short, and stiff, and the plant has an erect, wiry habit, the spreading branches often red brown to purplish in hue. But the asters are noted for their variability, even within species, and the plants often hybridize.

This leads to perhaps the oddest feature of the serpentine aster at Soldiers Delight. For while it is rare (botantists often come from far away to see it), few people know how to recognize it with certainty. Adding to the problems already mentioned, there are at least two other aster species in the area with nearly identical features. They grow in dry soils, have linear leaves, bushy habits, and small, many-rayed white flowers that appear in late summer. According to Clyde Reed, serpentine aster usually appears at Soldiers Delight in a sizeable clump, and loses its basal and lower leaves some time during late summer. Meanwhile, Wayne Tyndall, a state ecologist, says the chief diagnostic features appear in the flowers and flower-bracts, which are markedly smaller than those of its several look-alikes. Since Wayne believes that perhaps 90 percent of the bare ground asters at Soldiers Delight are *A. depauperatus*, it was probably this rare species that I noticed today by the overlook, scattered drably on the slopes.

More obvious at present is Indian grass, throughout the regions of serpentine. It stands in scattered bunches among the dry slopes or down beside the streams. By the wet spot next to Chimney Branch a few clumps are six feet tall, and, when examined closely, the varied colors in the ears—purple, buff, greenish—are some of its finest features. Henry David Thoreau, in his *Journals,* refers to "rye-and-Indian" loaves, suggesting that Indian grass was once used by Americans in their bread. But he calls the genus *Sorghum,* not *Sorghastrum* as it is classed today. Confusing this grass with the sorghums, which sometimes contain prussic acid and have been known to poison cattle, may have led early settlers to stop using it as human food. Still, the Indians probably ate it for centuries, and they definitely used it as a liner in the holes they dug to store corn, for Peter Kalm describes this technique in his eighteenth-century diaries.

Also by the wet spot was a great glaucous clump of big bluestem, or turkeyfoot, whose two- and three-parted ears, branched like the foot of a turkey, hung trembling in the breeze. Big bluestem, though often mentioned in conjunction with little bluestem, is not common at Soldiers Delight. It appears here and there in isolation, among wetter or richer soil pockets, achieving nothing like the rampant expanses that made it famous on the early "tall-grass prairies" of the deep-loamed Midwest.

Many purple gerardia by the stream were a full two feet tall, with deep belled flowers, their throats purple-freckled and twin-striped with custard yellow, and further adorned with tonguelike pistils and the multiple mustaches of pubescent, cream-colored anthers. Both slender and sandplain gerardia, up on the barrens, sported smaller blossoms of paler pink, some shading almost to white. Indeed, I have now come across purely white-flowered forms of both purple and slender gerardia near here, the latter having light green, almost chartreuse foliage, in contrast to its otherwise dark or reddish stems and branches.

Among gerardia, the size and shape of the calyx is the chief diagnostic feature, and the differences are in millimeters and degrees of angles. But with the known species at Soldiers Delight I've noted some details that, less technically, may aid identification: purple gerardia is the tall, long-branched, big-belled *Agalinis* of the floodplains, and its flower stems are short. It shares, with slender gerardia, both a tendency toward purple foliage, and toward arching its corollan lobes. However, slender gerardia, in addition, tolerates high, dry slopes, is smaller overall, and displays (not mentioned in the field guides) an extended style—that long center tube of the pistil—which curves out well beyond the bell like the whitened tongue of a serpent. Meanwhile, the globally rare *A. acuta*, scorning all but the driest areas, has no outsized style, has a paler and more delicate foliage, and is thinner and lower to the ground. Its shallow-belled, smallish flower is light pink, short-stemmed, and quite furry within, the lobes rarely arching, but spreading perpendicular to their base, like the brim of an old straw boater.

An eastern garter snake (*Thamnophis sirtalis sirtalis*) crossed the road as I drove away from the overlook, and an oncoming pickup swerved in trying to kill it. The snake speeded up in the last few seconds and barely escaped. Just another day, I suppose, in the life of a hated viper, whether harmless or not.

September 7

A fine late summer day full of sunlight and blue skies. I walked the east end of the northwest sector with Donna. The spicebush by the streams has already set its bright red berries. In the low, wet grass were visible the irregular webs of funnel weaver spiders (family *Agelenidae*). These creatures lurk beneath a hole at the back of each web, coming forth to check out vibrations. The webs are so numerous as to present a patchwork effect on some hillsides, their dew-soaked silvery nets showing plainly against the drab.

All three species of gerardia were evident here, and, in the floodplain of a little Mill Run tributary, purple gerardia was tangled low on its stems amid striking clumps of Indian grass.

Each day the gerardia drop their blossoms to the ground, often before noon. I have pondered why they should do this. Noting the fuzzy male anthers attached inside the corolla and the long style of the female pistil, I conclude that this seemingly senseless oddity, like so many in nature, has something to do with sex. The falling blossom is caught, however briefly, on the bending style, and rough anther chafes against stretched-out pistil, ensuring fertilization. Indeed, I once found a blossom detached from its nubby calyx, yet unable to drop quite free, and restrained instead—perhaps for hours—by the lanky but supportive style, like a great gaudy bracelet a-dangle on a slender arm.

September 8

Sunny and not quite hot. In the morning Donna and I tried the trails near the Locust Run cove. A young dog broke loose from a tether by Mr. Linthicum's mailbox and approached us with puppyish enthusiasm. We walked it up the driveway to his house and knocked on his big white door. As we waited, a bluebird pair flitted back and forth in the tree beside his porch. The squire himself appeared at last, in robe and slippers, to announce that the dog was not his, only briefly tethered out front (where someone had abandoned it) until his son could take it to the pound. He thanked us anyway, and the dog whined and the bluebirds fluttered as we made our way back to the woods.

It is not only the time of ripe grasses but of ripe berries as well. Along the trail above the lake we saw many red fruits of jack-in-the pulpit, in their tight bunches near the ground, and of flowering dogwood and spicebush. The blue-black berries of maple-leaf viburnum were also evident.

Of blooming wildflowers there were jewelweed, Asiatic dayflower (*Commelina communis*), great lobelia (*Lobelia siphilitica*), and a long bank of scarlet cardinal flower (*Lobelia cardinalis*) by the dry shore of the cove. The cove itself is empty but for the narrow channel of Locust Run whose languid flow finally merges with a shallow bay near the point. The main beaver lodge—largest of three—is now fully exposed and twenty yards from water, while the cove bottom is a vast meadow of sedges. These are mostly umbrella sedge (*Cyperus* species), of several varieties. The landscape here is utterly changed from that of April, and a visitor shown first one and later the other might think them different locations.

September 10

Rain threatened at midmorning, then faded. I walked west and north from the glades above Ward's Chapel Road, toward the fish pond. Little bluestem protrudes among the outcrops, showing now its small-tufted seed heads, while low in the lanes between the pine groves float the flat, pale clouds of boneset.

Near the pond, drought has reduced the hardwood forest undergrowth to a shedding sparseness and premature decay. The grove of black locust there has gone dusty gray brown, and closeup examination reveals leaves stripped to their lacy skeletons by the locust leaf miner (*Xenochalepus dorsalis*).

The destructive work of this insect is also apparent along many of our state highways where hillsides of infected black locust are a common sight.

The skulking ability of small birds in fall—and not merely migrants—is remarkable. There is much chipping and twittering amid the bushes and brambles but little visible bird. Through patience, however, I managed to find thirty-one species in less than two hours this morning, largely with the help of a small warbler flock that included black-and-white, black-throated blue, magnolia, and parula warblers, as well as yellowthroats, redstarts, and a red-eyed vireo. This is typical of fall birding. Many habitats will be quite dead—that is, empty of birds—until a small "hotspot" is reached, where, for reasons of favorable warmth or forage, or factors more cryptic, small birds of mixed species are so numerous that a single pair of eyes seem maddeningly inadequate.

September 15

Cloudy and humid. Donna and I walked toward the old quartz mill in the far upper corner of the northwest sector. Goldenrod and green foxtail were common beside the fields. Fraser and his helpers have collected the mass of hard trash near there into neat piles for pickup and disposal.

Along Mill Run there were many fallen acorns, much lovely jewelweed in shades from yellow to red orange, and scarlet leaves of black tupelo, or black gum, floating in the stream. A red maple has fallen across the boulders beside the mill, and has cluttered the largest pool. We rested and listened to the water. This was once a busy spot full of shouts and the noise of machines. Human clamor and busyness puts some people at ease. I prefer such places as relics and the sounds of wild nature to those of man.

While returning I noticed how many mushrooms have dried up or dessicated in the drought, or been eaten back to their bases. Some were poisonous *Amanitas,* and once again I wondered about the mechanism that makes palatable to other creatures what is deadly to human beings.

The woods were very quiet; crows cawed overhead, and a single blue jay squealed.

September 18

It rained hard last night; low gray clouds hemmed the valleys in the middle sector this morning, and below them numbers of chimney swifts swooped and dodged.

I observed that the dominant bloom in the glades above Chimney Branch these days is the diminutive gray goldenrod. This inhabitant of serpentine and old fields tends to form flowered plumes on one side only, especially near its crest, and sprouts small leaflets where the main leaves join the stem. Two other goldenrod species, early goldenrod (*Solidago juncea*) and lance-leaved goldenrod (*Solidago graminifolia*), are more common outside the glades.

The first fringed gentians (*Gentianopsis crinita*) have risen beside the stream and are very near to blooming, their dark blue petals still twisted into a closed spike an inch or so high, yet with frayed edges poised to spiral open on the square, green clasp of the sepal. Normally plants of the mountain foothills or the cooler North, they are almost never found this far south in either the Piedmont or the Coastal Plain and currently exist nowhere else in Maryland.

Meanwhile, New York aster (*Aster novae-belgii*), in shades from white to pink to blue, is blooming on the slopes and in low tangles beside the stream trail.

The entire region below the power-cut has been recently mowed, wasting the budding grove of quaking aspen. Worse still, a large swath along the Chimney Branch floodplain, where some of the finest purple gerardia and fringed gentians were blooming or set to bloom, was cut flat. This is the result of allowing the local power company to hire their own botanically ignorant contractors for the job, a practice that has gone on for years.

Spared, however, was a lovely adjacent glade of little bluestem, Indian grass, gray goldenrod, serpentine aster, sandplain gerardia, grass-leaved blazing-star, and purplish three-awn (*Aristida purpurascens*). This little autumn prairie remnant—with its splashes of pink, yellow, and white and its subtle, earthy ground-tones—is a good example of what is fine and rich in the area's rocky openings. Around it, sloping up or down, are hillsides of oak and pungent pine, quilted beneath by moss and lichen, and by prickly, bright green mats of moss-phlox.

I rested here a moment. A big Cooper's hawk came up over the trees—soaring, flapping, soaring—and was harassed at intervals by a growing storm of chimney swifts, now fully risen from their nighttime roosts to continue their southward migration.

Walking back past the Visitor Center I found a flock of five eastern phoebes—perhaps a family group—darting and resting, tails a-wag, in the low blackjack oaks. And a palm warbler, deeply dipping its tail and yellow rump, confronted me in a piney glade a short ways from my car.

September 24

This morning I decided to search the eastern sector for both gerardia and fringed gentians. Purple gerardia I could not find at all in this region, though *A. tenuifolia* or *A. acuta* occasionally dotted damp places along the trails. The fringed gentian was even scarcer. In fact I found it at only one location in the whole sector, on the banks of Red Run. And even there I discovered but one plant, graced with three or four half-open blooms.

Meanwhile, dense blazing-star, gray goldenrod, and serpentine aster proliferate in the glades, stippling them with color on even dark days like this one.

In the northwest part of this sector is a place where the transition from prairie glades to rich woodlands is abrupt—a sloping descent of fifty yards, through a thin grove of pines, takes one off the barrens onto a lush floodplain. Beside Red Run here, I took my coffee.

As I sat down, a small southern leopard frog (*Rana utricularia*) jumped into the clear, shallow water at my feet. Though I saw exactly where it entered, I couldn't find it until I turned over a stone. It quickly shot under another stone, and when I turned that one over, too, it lay motionless while I gazed at the lovely brown-on-olive blotches of its back, contained by the salmon-buff lines of its raised dorsal folds. It soon swam off very deftly with smooth kicks of its leopard-spotted legs. The fingers of the frog's smaller forelegs—when it stopped to raise them beside a dark twig—looked like the rays of a tiny starfish, impossibly delicate, palely suspended in a limpid pool.

September 27

A shining fall day! In the eastern end of the northwest sector, fringed gentian is now blooming beside one of the Mill Run tributaries. Nearby is a small ridge covered with lichens, especially the gray, coral-like branches of reindeer lichen.

Along the steep bank there, a type of peat moss (*Sphagnum* species) has formed a very thick carpet. I plunged a thin stick into its center to a depth of one foot. This is typical of *Sphagnum*, which, combining small green leaf cells with large dead ones, may form deep, water-retaining mats not only in bogs and ponds, but in ditches, along banksides, and on wet, acid soils. It is normally associated with cooler, wetter regions north and west. The species here is almost certainly *Sphagnum capillaceum*, which Clyde Reed described as growing with *Gentianopsis crinita*, in a "boggy area" along this creek.

Purplish three-awn is now prime in many of the glades, and beyond them, up toward the fish pond, the hips of multiflora rose and the fruits of wild grape have come ripe. The former cluster like scarlet beads on the great thorny tangles, while the latter hang in dusty blue clumps wherever their vines have stationed them to take the autumn sun. I tasted a few of the larger grapes, which were sour but not unpalatable, the pulp a deep tongue-staining magenta and the several large pips like shiny little beetles when I spit them into the sun.

Above the Stivers house, on a hill overlooking the glades to the east, is a region of dead trees—mostly pines—perhaps two acres in size. It is nothing but woody skeletons, in contrast to the green all around. I discussed this once with Fraser Bishop, and it may be the result of dumped chemicals, as the former resident was a printer who stored solvents in drums nearby. Perhaps the temptation to "liquidate" his hazardous inventory, in the great tradition of American waste disposal, was too strong.

Since the recent rains, many mushrooms have cropped up in the woods near here: mostly stark-white amanitas—some eight inches tall—with broad umbrella caps. Walnuts are dropping their big green nut-balls on the paths nearby, and I spotted a broken white bird's egg in a trail through the fields, perhaps that of a pheasant.

Back toward the old chromite mill foundation, in a feral orchard above Mill Run, I found a single fruitful apple tree, its orange globes dangling in the sunlight and visible from the trail. The apple skins were scarred and bumpy, but the flesh of one I picked was crisp, white, and pleasantly tart. I ate it down to the core.

Returning to the trail, I flushed a woodcock from the bramble and scrub, and three deer bounded past near the old sluice mill. This marks the ninth straight outing that I've got at least a glimpse of white-tailed deer, and you could count on both hands the number of times I've missed them since the new year.

September 29

Again I walked a circuit into the northwest sector, this time with Donna, beginning in the east end glades north of Ward's Chapel.

The fabled fringed gentians are at peak bloom, standing several feet tall beside the streams. It is little wonder that this species is celebrated in story and verse. The fringed, ultramarine petals are soft and finely tattered at their flared tips, like abraded feather-ends from some small blue bird, drawn together into an upright tube or bell over an inch deep. Within this tube they are lovelier still, shooting violet pin stripes up the interior lining from a luminous chartreuse base. The slender center pistil, like some minute Venetian bottle, is palest green, and is clasped vertically by the lavender ribs of the stamen, which ascend toward the lemon stigma and its tight orbit of saffron anthers.

In one particular area of exposed serpentinite streambed—where the reddish black outcrops rise in humpy slabs and benches—the gentians seem sprung from the rock itself. The poor conditions inhibit their growth, yet they somehow get a root-hold in detritus-filled cracks and crannies, and send up their pale green stems and leaves to heights of less than a foot. Indeed, many here are fantastic miniatures. Half-size flowers bloom atop four- and five-inch stalks, and I have found several viable plants—their blossoms well formed—whose total height from stem-base to flower-tip was barely over an inch. To the best of my knowledge, these tiny *Gentianopsis crinita*—growing from the rock outcrops themselves and only one to two inches tall—have never been described before at Soldiers Delight or elsewhere. Perhaps, like some of the gerardia, they only germinate once every few years. It seems unlikely that they represent a genetic divergence, but at the very least they are an interesting example of dwarfism, or "nanism," as some botanists call it, for the normal height of this species is one to three feet.

We found many webs of funnel weaver spiders near the ground here. One of the tiny eighth-inch arachnids came forward from his lair when I jostled the web with my finger.

Some Virginia creeper (*Parthenocissus quinquefolia*) has gone burnt red, as has sassafras and staghorn sumac.

A pleasant discovery, which somehow eluded me before, was of Chinese chestnut trees (*Castanea mollissima*) near the fish pond, low-crowned and hoary-barked, whose many prickly nut-husks are dispelling their flat-sided fruits. The "chestnut"-colored shell of these nuts, which were scattered by the trail, resembles the finest wood veneer, and the meat is sweet and delicious. We collected several dozen.

We also raided my "wild" apple tree nearby and partook of the flawless apple flesh well-disguised by the ugly skins.

There is mustiness in the air, the hillocks are dry and tangled and ripe with subtle tones, and the old-gold light of autumn is starting to seep and spill.

September 30

Sunny and cool. I found magnolia warblers beside Chimney Branch in the middle sector, frisking in the pines. The fringed gentians extend for half a mile along this stream, and blue-white New York asters are everywhere on the grassy banks, scattered like fallen stars.

To the north, near the power-cut, a small area of fire-charred oaks and pines—some of them fifty feet tall—is already recarpeted at its base with composites, goldenrods, greenbriar, and tall brown spikes of dried common mullein (*Verbascum thapsus*). Blueberry leaves near the glades are showing rust and cinnamon and, occasionally—where sunlight strikes them from behind—a luminous red.

October *Tinted Woodlands*

White Russala

Fringed Gentian

Long-tailed Salamander

October 2

Last Sunday, Jim Flater came by to examine my Indian artifacts. He was recommended by the state archeologist as someone to contact for their verification. There were about ten pieces that he could say for sure had been worked by Indians, including a stone chopper that I myself had had doubts about.

So this morning I brought the artifacts over to Fraser Bishop for the last time, where he can now display them at the Visitor Center. The Center is finally open part time—three days a week—though the official dedication is not until November.

I walked up toward the fish pond in the fine autumn sunshine and stopped to gather chestnuts again. There are actually four Chinese chestnut trees here, three of them quite large, and they were no doubt planted originally—like the apple trees—by the former owner of the property. The trees will not produce without cross-pollination, so several are always needed. There were many deer droppings in among the fallen fruits; I suspect deer break the husks with their hooves to get at the savory nuts. After stowing my bag of nuts in the car, I headed south from Ward's Chapel, along a flat serpentine plain in the middle sector that was once a race course and trash dump. Just beyond this, along a main tributary of Chimney Branch, were many fine fringed gentians. I even found one blooming in the middle of a dry trail. An extended wet area here, marked by a rusting car body, is full of gentians and gerardia, until the sunlight gives way to greenbriar. Above one bank was a huge mushroom—the short-stalked white russula (*Russula brevipes*)—with a cap nine inches across.

October 4

A lulling fall day, full of warm drafts, fat clouds, and ripe colors. In afternoon I headed out the farm road in the northwest sector, to a woodland trail where I found that stone chopper last spring. On a hunch that there might be others, I poked around by the eroded path but found nothing of interest.

While returning I stopped on a hill to take in the farmland vista: mowed hayfields below me were rimmed by colored edges and borders with tinted woodlands beyond, and the sky moved vaguely with summer clouds. The two seasons had collided.

Migrating tree swallows swooped briefly against the blue before seeming to melt away. Errant blue jays came over in groups—six here, seven there, then a flock of twenty-five, with one breaking ranks above me to snatch some sort of insect. Sassafras and dogwood burned in the brushy edges, a net of creeper glowed scarlet, and crickets laid down their rhythms—continuous or interrupted—on the sultry, hay-scented air. The peace and well-being of childhood was about, the after-school autumn quiet—as brief and illusory now as it was then, but just as delicious.

October 5

Elmer Worthley's memorial service began about 11:15 behind Red Dog Lodge. Most of his children spoke, and several friends. The day had cleared off nicely from a foggy, misting start.

The long westward vista behind the group showed the hills of Carroll County—Elmer's last place of residence—hazed softly under the sun, while the compact foreground of the lodge was ringed with blackjack and post oak, whose leathery leaves shuffled with each breeze.

The singing of "Annie Laurie" was especially poignant, the voices of the shy, awkward mourners, who perched on stiff little chairs, somehow transcending their unpretty physical presence, so that, with eyes closed, one heard only the sad Celtic whisper of the tune, soft and high and pure, as if from the throats of children. When the last line ended, "I'd lay me down and dee," the breeze stiffened sharply in the oaks, and a red-tailed hawk was visible, high up, tracing circles against the blue.

October 7

A bright cool morning in the eastern sector. A small flock of Canada geese flew over, but because I had entered the pine and oak woods I could not see them, only hear their wonky cries. This somehow increased their appeal.

There are some large post oaks here, sixty to seventy feet tall, and three feet thick at their bases. I sat down where a small chestnut oak was dropping oblong yellow-green acorns with maroon tips, nearly all devoid of their rough brown caps. I looked up to see the caps still attached to their separate twigs, high in the crown.

Fallen pine trees here, half decayed, score the dry ground like low gray-green benches, their color supplied by a full coat of verdant lichens—pyxie cups and British soldiers mostly—with occasional badges of lime green moss. I heard a single red-breasted nuthatch calling—*neet-neet*—from somewhere nearby; they have returned to their winter quarters here.

In the Red Run floodplain, the bankside understory has gone yellow with spicebush. Red maples are spilling green and scarlet leaves in the stream, which glistens on its sunlit course over stones and leaf-dams of brown, ocher, and red.

Skunk cabbage has shrunk to tuliplike bulb spikes in the wet deltas, and eastern crayfish burrows are mounded about with muddy spoils. A garden slug occupied one such tunnel.

A rope was added, probably last summer, above the swimming hole by the big dead oak. I stopped there for coffee and watched the blue sky over the hayfields in the distance. On the way back I found many gem-studded puffballs (*Lycoperdon perlatum*)—choicely edible little whitish mushrooms—scattered under the river birches (*Betula nigra*). I carefully picked just a few to include in tonight's supper.

October 11

This morning I finished my Soldiers Delight cumulative bird list, printed it out, and dropped it off at Fraser's. The breeding bird total stands at 81 species—a figure that will probably not go much higher—while migrants bring the grand total thus far to 132 species, and this last should increase all the time.

I made a quick visit to the northwest sector, just past the Weir Mine off Ward's Chapel Road. It was cloudy and still and threatening rain, with a lemon sun glowing briefly through the gray. Crickets and crows seemed the only sound until I got into a tangled grove south of Mill Run. Here a blue jay scolded, a Carolina wren chattered, and northern flickers flew back and forth in the gloom ahead, calling *wick-a, wick-a, wick,* and flashing the gold of their wings.

I saw two warbler species: a black-throated green some distance away, and a drab young yellow-rumped, darting about in the branches overhead with the nervousness of a flycatcher. A solitary vireo—with bluish head and fine white spectacles—posed a moment, while robins and cardinals fed on bowers of grapes. The sky lowered, and a chill breeze rose, spitting drops of tiny rain.

October 14

A clear, crisp fall day. Walking the eastern sector, I found that more gem-studded puffballs, surprisingly, have come up in the center of a main trail through the barrens.

This being Columbus Day holiday, there were more visitors about than I find enjoyable. A hostile growl greeted me at one leafy trail-bend, and a big dog ran toward me. I soothed him with firm passivity, and the couple responsible looked on sheepishly from a distance, leash in hand. There are few things so annoying outdoors as having one's peace of mind jarred by such thoughtless hikers, who, like people with spoiled children, think the rules don't apply to *their* pets. The leash law in Baltimore County, as I then loudly explained, protects not only *people* from rude and risky intrusion, but, more especially, guards ground-nesting birds and small mammals, many of whose numbers are dwindling. When an unleashed dog leaves the path, as they invariably do, to "innocently" sniff out a nest, it leaves a telltale scent-trail that is later followed by foxes, raccoons, skunks, or opossums, who—unlike the dreamy, well-fed dogs—make short work of their quarries.

Golden-crowned kinglets have arrived, and it struck me that the way they move in the trees, often dropping and fluttering down through the branches, mimics the fall of dead leaves. I twice mistook bird for leaf, and vice versa, while watching.

Beside Red Run a yellow-billed cuckoo flew up from the bushes, and a Swainson's thrush, with its distinctive buffy eye-ring, perched motionless nearby. White-throated sparrows have also arrived; a small flock played hide-and-seek in a streamside clump of spicebush.

It was two years ago that I saw the young golden eagle in this part of Soldiers Delight. Today the dead and fallen tree where he once roosted was dabbed with bright fungi, especially the little orange stems called clammy caloceras (*Calocera viscosa*), which resemble vivid corals. A strange bark fungus of chocolate-pink, much like paint or spilled cocoa, was smeared along one bough.

Red Run itself was low and riffly here, full of green-husked walnuts—nearly tennis-ball size—and of leaves, fractured quartz and serpentinite, and glistening sunlight. I could hear a farmer mowing his hayfields to the north. When I paused going back, to watch from the woods, I saw a brazen red fox, one ear cocked toward the combine over the hill, sniffing and searching the just-cut rye for windfall rodents or insects.

Most of the blazing-star in the glades have set tufts of flat, brownish seeds, up and down their dark dry stems. Yet a few are still in full purplish bloom.

October 18

Yesterday was a wild, blustery day of rain and cold, and today was as much its opposite as one might ever expect: sunny, still, and with the air warming into the seventies after noon.

In the northwest sector, by the farm road, the apricot-orange fruits of a leafless persimmon stood out against the sky. The flowering dogwoods along the field edge here were brilliant in the bright sun: scarlet berries in bunches against oxblood leaves.

In the trail I discovered three shiny quarters—one after the other as in a money-finding dream—which someone had dropped. It occurred to me that the buying power of one quarter today is roughly the same as that of the 1835 "large cent"—which I found here last April—in its day.

In the woods above Mill Run lovely yellow and brown mats of tulip-tree, shagbark hickory, red oak, spicebush, and sassafras leaves—wet and glossy from the rain—covered the forest floor. The hay-scented fern has gone buffy, contrasting neatly with the deep green of abundant Christmas fern, whose frond-ends are covered below with bran-colored spore cases, or "sori."

Nearby I found what looked like a pileated woodpecker nest hole—large and oval in shape—near the top of a thirty-foot oak snag, and framed above and below by hat-size clumps of a strange polypore mushroom (family *Polyporaceae*), resembling au gratin potatoes. The residing woodpeckers may be the same that have heavily excavated a tree trunk up the trail.

Yellow and suffused green are the colors of the canopy today, with the deepest sky-blue background. Circling toward home I heard from afar the muffled *clop-clop* of a busy pileated woodpecker, and, approaching quietly, saw the female patiently chopping big chips from a dead limb. Strange that I just wrote a story about this muted pileated chopping sound and earlier found my first nest hole in that part of Soldiers Delight. Until today, I had not even *seen* the species this well in perhaps five or six months.

October 21

Sunny and cold. The first light frost of fall. I looked for long-tailed salamanders at the Choate Mine again, without success.

This is one of the prettiest and most graceful salamander species that I know of. The tail is extended and whiplike, its length from behind the rear legs to its tip being greater than that of its body. Its ground color may vary from yellow to orange brown or red, though the ones I have seen in this region are a rich caramel above and yellowish below, with dark, broken vertical bars on the tail and lateral brown flecks stretching forward to the eye. The wonderful glistening skin has a pliant smoothness and amber patina, faintly suggesting, with its chocolate-flaked caramel tones, some exotic French toffee sculpted in amphibian form.

I was recently privileged to hold a sleek trio of these creatures in my hand while visiting Jean Worthley's home. The springhouse beside her lower pond is a veritable long-tail paradise, damp and cool and protected, the gurgle and drip of water affording ceaseless music, while fifteen or twenty of these salamanders haunt a large, loose cover of concrete blocks. "Hold" is not the right word for what I did, as I never quite clutched them, merely let them explore my open palm, canter alertly in slow-motion bursts along the warm bough of my wrist, or squeeze through the delta of my half-spread fingers, their bodies glinting as I stepped into the sunlight.

There is something in the touch of their splayed, fine-formed fingers, the tips delicate and round, that reminds one of the patty-cake grope of a crib-bound human infant, while the tail is wielded in the otter's way, with casualness and purpose both, and the blunt shiny nose and bulging eyes evoke some naive puppy. Familiar in all these ways, cobbled to sight and mind like a tinker toy of remembrance, yet they are utterly strange, exactly like nothing but themselves, wild things from a hidden realm who duplicate no form on earth.

The fringed gentians along Chimney Branch, already much reduced in bloom, are almost finished, many of the larger flower-heads sheathed in dry brownish petals, and the leaves gone waxy yellow green. The once lovely blossoms have closed around the fat capsule of the pistil, which is full of green or—in drier specimens—black seeds. Perhaps a third of the gentian blooms still survive, while I saw nothing of the gerardias.

I stopped by the Visitor Center on my way back and was told by Fraser that a "prescribed burn" was planned for noon, up in the east end of the northwest sector. Fire is a natural component of the original prairie ecosystem, which is the main reason for the burns. By employing prescribed burns, incursions of woody plants are curtailed and, in addition, the precise botanical way in which these prairies recover from fire can be studied. Usually there are two or three adjacent study sites of similar plant composition. One, the control, remains unburned, while the others are burned at varying intervals.

Wayne Tyndall, an ecologist with the Maryland Natural Heritage Program, first burned a "black line"—a perimeter scorching—around the site to be set afire, with the help of local firemen and volunteers. This is achieved, like the burn itself, by using a propane torch. About 12:45 the main burn was started, but due to frail winds and too much residual ground moisture, it couldn't sustain itself. The burn was rescheduled for another time, much to the disappointment of onlookers, myself, and a TV crew included. Still, one got the general idea, as big tufts of Indian grass and little bluestem were set blazing by the torch. The smell of charred grass was nostalgic, recalling the odor of those "accidental" vacant-lot grass fires in my childhood.

At Soldiers Delight prescribed burns are useful for Wayne's plant studies and for scorching unwanted tree seedlings in the remaining glades. Indeed, fire is often essential for maintaining an open, healthy prairie. It purges mats of sun-blocking dead matter and releases important nutrients to the soil, allowing grasses to come back thick and strong. But by itself fire cannot eliminate established forest intrusions. Even the best burn only blackens the lower trunks of Virginia pines, whose sparse branches start higher up and do not easily ignite. Barring a huge conflagration, only continued cutting will beat back mature stands of nuisance trees that continue to develop.

October 23

To the northwest sector. Morning fog erased everything by the path but bird and cricket calls, and the noise of phantom gray squirrels. Common milkweed pods have burst, like grotesque quivers, half spilling the tight bundles of silk-shafted "arrows" with their blunt-seeded tips.

As the fog lifted slightly, a red-eyed vireo was singing as late in the season as I've ever heard one, while yellow-rumped warblers and ruby-crowned kinglets chased about in tree and bush.

A strong, sour smell, as of decayed apples and horse dung,

was evident on the road near the pasture. Diffuse flocks of American robins chuckled in the field edges and quarreled over berries. The Chinese chestnuts have dropped all their husked fruits and gone leathery tan and gold. Nearby, under scrubby pines, large panther amanitas (*Amanita velatipes*)—yellow and orange with pale freckles—have risen in scattered formations, some bulbous and emergent, others older and topped with saucer-size caps. Many have been nibbled or trampled.

The sun broke through by the pond, awakening great colored maples and poplars and rubbing blue patches through the sky. On the pond surface, which was still as gelatin, leaves fluttered and landed, affixing their concentric seals. A belted kingfisher rattled. Young frogs burrowed into the silt as I sat down by the shore. At the pond's far end a covey of five wood ducks—led by a brilliant male with cream white eyebrows—left the exposed shoreline and swam, bobbing alertly, deep into the cattails.

I sat completely still and emptied my mind of thought.

October 25

Foggy again. Above the prairies of the northwest and middle sectors, hillsides of strong orange and yellow held a muted luster through the white mists.

Despite media predictions to the contrary, the long summer drought has produced an autumn of colorful leafy splendor. Carotenoids, xanthophylls, and anthocyanins, those accessory leaf pigments to green chlorophyll which provide the fall oranges, yellows, and reds, exist partly to absorb light of different wavelengths, and thus aid chlorophyll in its short season of converting photoenergy. They are all present—contrary to common belief—in summer leaves. The presence of some, especially the scarlet and purple anthocyanins, increases with cooler weather, but none are produced solely in the fall. They are simply revealed then as chlorophyll is destroyed.

Chlorophyll begins to decay in autumn. Most of the minerals and organic compounds it has converted from light energy have been transferred to the roots and trunk for winter storage. While chlorophyll decays quickly, the other pigments are more stable, and, in the absence of chlorophyll's green, are plainly seen.

Anthocyanins—common in the maples, dogwoods, sumacs, and oaks—increase with cold and dryness, conditions that also favor sugar production. Summer drought may tend to concentrate sugar in trees—just as it does in some fruits—and, because trees make anthocyanin from sugar, lead to high fall levels of this pigment. This would be news to the local media, however, who consulted various "experts" and concluded that drought would mean dull foliage.

October 27

I could not help but contemplate anthocyanins again this morning, for, in the eastern sector where Donna and I began our walk, the blueberry leaves were scarlet and maroon with these pigments, in excess even of their August vividness.

Through these shrubs—not fifteen yards ahead and directly across our path—came crashing at full sprint a big muscular doe. Neither of us had seen a deer at flat-out gallop this close before. She barreled forward in a low posture, in the manner of some charging lion or panther, and was sporting the grayish brown winter coat that replaces the chestnut of summer. Whatever scared her so—probably dogs, for we met several unleashed "pets" later on—did not pursue her.

The paths and woodlands further on were chock-full of fallen leaves, and of the sour-must smell that comes with them. Donna collected the prettiest discards—two-toned maple leaves of crimson and gold, yellow mittens of sassafras, purple-lobed oaks, tan and ocher poplars—into a thick little palette of colors. Of course they will soon curl and fade but are fun to scatter on the porch at home, in a circle around our fat pumpkin.

October 29

Clear and cold. The foot-high path rush (*Juncus tenuis*) has matured everywhere on the trails in the eastern sector. This is one of the few true rushes (family *Juncaceae*) at Soldiers Delight (bulrush—*Scirpus* species—found by some creeks, is actually a sedge), having, unlike sedges, a single pouch holding all its seeds. An innocuous plant, yet its toughness defies credulity, the jointless stems protruding from cementlike soil. In fact it seems to prefer the most hard-packed trails, which are without much competition, yet open to some sunlight—a difficult niche which the plant has evolved to exploit.

I made a final check for long-tailed salamanders at a rocky spring beside Red Run but fear it is now too cold.

The big-toothed aspen were stripped of their foliage in last night's wind, leaving polelike pale gray trunks that shone in the sun, while a few copper wind chimes of clustered leaves still vibrated near their crowns.

In a pine grove nearby I flushed either a Cooper's or sharp-shinned hawk, I could not tell which. He landed deeper in the trees and watched me with a bright red eye before flying off through the woods.

The oak grove past the pines was especially lovely, despite damage by gypsy moths. Deep-lobed leaves were suffused to translucence by sunlight, their tones of amber and pomegranate aquiver against the blue. Fire-red black tupelo and flowering dogwood flickered in the understory. The tupelos were further embellished with dark clusters of grapelike fruits, and both robins and cedar waxwings busily worked to devour them.

As I came out on Sunnyking Drive near the sector's northeast corner, I watched two woodchucks—one on either side of the road—bask and scurry in the fields. Despite the lateness of the season, the sun was so strong that it hurt my unshielded eyes.

I ended up at the old oak above Red Run. A collapsed pokeweed stalk there—an inch thick and shiny magenta—looked from a distance like some store-bought item, some lacquered rod or bike-bar.

Though their fruits have been formed for some time, an absence of leaves on the sycamores makes their cherry-bomb seed balls appear freshly hung out.

I drank my coffee looking skyward, with my back against the trunk. The air smelled faintly of smoke and the crisp, cold breeze was full of the Midwest. As I hiked back, a winter wren surprised me by the trail—the first I have seen this season—darting out along a log in a brief aggressive sortie, then plunging off its far end and never reappearing.

November *A Strangeness in the Air*

Greenbriar and
Sphagnum Moss

Tuliptree

American Woodcock

November 1

This month I've decided to explore those few obscure places at Soldiers Delight to which I've never been. Now that many of the plants and vines have died back, access should be easier. I began this morning from a road behind Fraser's house in the middle sector. Not fifty yards down the trail a four-point buck charged by me and vanished into the woods. I hiked up under the power lines, then south down the steep slope to Locust Run.

Eastern bluebirds were about, perching on the lowest wires, and two red-tailed hawks sat on the steel pylons past the stream, now and then uttering their *keeer-r-r-r!* call. Some bluebirds will overwinter here, and the hawks are probably migrants from further north, who will spend the winter nearby. There is no way of telling for sure. Displacement of hawk populations, after breeding, takes place in a general north-to-south flow, but whether these two have come from Maine, or New York State, or Pennsylvania, or merely from Harford County, is impossible to say, and they could end up in Virginia or the Carolinas before the winter is through.

I turned east to the far southern boundary—again marked by yellow tree blazes—in the woods southeast of the pylons. Here I reversed to the northeast, upstream along a branch of Locust Run, and entered new territory.

There is an interesting hillside of strewn gabbro boulders to the west, their flanks covered with blue-gray lichens of the genus *Parmelia*. The little valley here is pretty, secluded despite proximity to houses, and at this point steep-sided, with mountain laurel greening the eastern slope, tall columns of tulip-tree and red oak, and, above the stream itself, the first flowers of witch-hazel (*Hammamelis virginiana*) that I've noticed this season.

The slender yellow petals of this fall-blooming tree or bush, arranged in twisted stars about an axil of greenish yellow bracts, appear on the bare twigs and branches, floating, it sometimes seems from a distance, in the air above the streams. To fanciful minds, the crimped whorl of petals may suggest lurid hair on a witch's chin or nose, but the name in fact stems from early settlers' use of the forked branches for divining underground water, a practice known as "witching." The Indians used witch-hazel's inner bark as a skin balm, which—in a dilute modern concoction—is its very use today.

Just upstream I found an old dry-stone wall, now pleasantly hoary with moss and lichens and feathered at its base with fronds of Christmas fern. Directly opposite, above the western stream bank, is perhaps the largest unbroken rock face in the park, a sheer vertical monolith, maybe twelve feet high and twenty feet across. Below it stands a tentlike natural structure formed of overlapping slabs. Such formations, known as shelter-rocks, or rock-shelters, were often used by native peoples while hunting or traveling, as protection against the elements.

The main stream channel here is blocked by a great jam of boulders, probably man-made, for to one side is evidence of a concrete housing and a system of pumps and pipes. I chatted with Fraser on my return, and he told me these were employed by the nearby well-less farmer, who used a mechanical "water-ram" to force water to his house directly from the stream, a practice known in the region until recent times.

November 3

Cool and windy, with clouds scudding from the northwest. Donna and I walked up past the pond and beside the pheasant enclosures. Broken white eggs in the trail here were clearly those of escapees.

Where the trail heads south again through the woods, the pits of an old quartz quarry—worn gouges in the leafy hillside—appear like shallow ravines. This was the Warner Quarry, named for a nearby farmer. In the early part of this century, quartz ore from this pit was hauled to a mill in Glen Morris, where the Maryland Quartz Company ground it into some twenty different crushed quartz products, used for everything from pottery glazes to poultry grit. Their commonest use was in sandpaper, of which there were many grades. This morning the fallen leaves near the quarry formed a crunchy carpet that made silent movement impossible.

Autumn leaves drop not because of frost but because the season stimulates the growth, across the base of the leaf stalk, of a protective cork layer. It is this cork seal that kills the leaf, and the date of its appearance varies by species. Tree types that have evolved in this latitude seal their leaf stalk bases early enough to protect against the usual arrival time of damaging cold weather. Transplants native to Europe and elsewhere, where winters are milder, have evolved to seal much later, here putting them at risk from early cold. Norway maples (*Acer platanoides*) are a good example. One in our backyard is still bright green, and will be for weeks, while trees around it have colored and mostly shed.

November 5

Sunny and cold—twenty-one degrees Fahrenheit at dawn. Our first hard frost.

I walked to the southeast corner of the northwest sector to the old pasture and creek bottom above Mr. Linthicum's place. The fields were dense with goldenrod, broken here and there by young Virginia pines and many escaped ornamentals, including cherry and apple trees, autumn olive, and flowering dogwoods now bright with berries. The creek bed was flat and dry, full of faded smartweed and pasture grass.

Further south the streambed steepens. Just past its main fork stands a massive tulip-tree, the largest I have seen at Soldiers Delight. It measured 162 inches (15½ feet) at chest height. Like others nearby, its topmost twigs are now filled with pale, erect seed clusters that closely resemble flowers.

I circled up to the pasture, where the goldenrod was four feet tall, densely formed, and crested with oatmeal-colored seed heads that shed cottony stars when even slightly brushed.

The soil here is loose in places; a woodchuck has burrowed at midfield, the tailings and damp tunnel being wholly of beach-grade sand.

I drank my coffee in a small clearing so thoroughly littered with walnuts—their husks blackened with frost—that it seemed impossible that the single tree beside me, just fifteen feet tall, could have dropped them all. Yet this was clearly the case.

I flushed a woodcock on the way back, his fat breast cinnamon in the sunlight as he flew.

November 6

There is one more place in the northwest sector that I've never explored, and today—in the cold bright morning—I decided to visit it. It appears as a narrow "panhandle" on maps, in the far north-central region.

I approached from the area of dead pines above the Stivers house. Here American bittersweet has entwined some of the stumps, its red berries mounted on the yellow-orange trefoils of open pods. Through the nearly leafless hardwoods to the east were visible pale patches of serpentine glades. Further on, among pines unaffected by whatever killed their neighbors, I found openings of matted grass where deer had recently bedded.

When the long grove of Virginia pines petered out, two elaborate deer stands or tree forts, inside a fence, marked the start of the panhandle. This thin strip of parkland is bounded by a farm on the west side and begins as a reclaimed field full of black walnut and boxelder (*Acer negundo*), becoming dense with greenbriar where the woods thicken toward the top.

I crossed a thin stream and, looking back, saw a big doe move away along the bank, picking her feet up daintily like someone traversing puddles in their best shoes.

The upper end was impassable with briars and edged by rusted farm trash. Through the thin pines to the west were visible barns and long pens of pheasants, who—like chickens—cackled with alarm at my approach. Here and there an escaped member of their band lay headless in the weeds, the victim of a fox, cat, or owl.

I found the whole panhandle ugly and retreated before too long. Under an old tire past the creek, where I stopped for a snack, was a dead red-backed salamander, which seemed to sum up my impressions.

Returning through the pine woods I found a patch of frost-killed pokeweed—most of it taller than my head and festooned with blackish fruit—standing among the trees. This was the best example of pokeweed's partial shade tolerance that I have yet seen. Some of the pines were nearly dead, so perhaps the thin branches had let in just enough summer light for this patch to thrive.

I descended eastward into a dry sloping region of prairie glades, recently swallowed by pines. There were many mound-building ant hills and clearings littered with serpentinite. Cutting across the barrens, I saw what looked like a cliff by a stream. I moved closer to discover an old dam of dry-stone construction, built entirely of serpentinite rocks. This is the dam that formed the pond for the downstream chromite mill, which today is nothing but a ruin, yet once probably served both the nearby Weir and Harris diggings. A millrace once tumbled west of here for perhaps three hundred yards but has vanished with little trace. The stream has since worked its way around this dam, leaving only a broad wet depression at its downstream base.

Today the hoary stone wall is just another ghostly remnant of the region's milling and mining days. Hardly more than an accent of ironic quiet and subtle beauty, its hard brow has been stripped of ambition's hat and covered instead by nature's own, a low fedora of lichen, moss, and woven grass, crushed down by time and neglect and softened by wind and rain.

November 9

Cold and raw. Donna and I cut southeast across the prairies from Ward's Chapel Road, in the middle sector. One of Wayne Tyndall's burn sites is here and an area he has cleared of mature pines. Only the three-foot stumps remain, amid a section of charred ground.

The hilly, open glades nearby provide nice vistas to the south and west, and big sky views. Today's was a winter sky, cold and slate gray, ruffled with pale scallops or cracked apart by blue, in splinters above the horizon. The wind cut us on the hilltops and bounced and fussed in the pines.

We climbed north under the power lines, crossed Ward's Chapel Road, and headed back west on deer trails through the scrub. Two white-taileds bounded away. I showed Donna the old stone dam to the northwest and a big mat of peat moss that has gone cranberry and maroon with the frost. Its surface maintains a soft pattern of tufted leaves, the whole of it like some antique upholstery, tinged and faded with Victorian reds. This variety seems to differ from the one I noted in September and is perhaps *Sphagnum palustre,* the form found in 1905 by Dr. C. C. Plitt, who led the Baltimore Botanic Club on forays here for nearly thirty-five years.

Donna spotted a single bright yellow goldenrod—spared from freezing by its shelter in the pines—not far from our parked car.

November 12

A cool, windy, half-sunny morning. There is but one place I have not explored in the middle sector this year, a region I call the Briar Patch, on the west side of the power-cut.

I followed the cut south to Locust Run, then went west and north through the hardwoods. Here European barberry (*Berberis vulgaris*)—a common escape in the woods and edges—stands out sharply at this season, with its oval, red-orange fruits aglow amid endless browns.

On a hill I rediscovered the little amphitheater of last winter, where the wren and thrush had cheered me amid thorns and cold. But this morning I was impatient, and, without finding the proper deer-trail exit, plunged north on a dead reckoning toward the branch of Locust Run that would be my pathway west. The greenbriar closed about me and the stream did not appear, at least not for a hundred yards or so, by which time I was scratched and sweaty and cursing the grip of "tramp's troubles."

The creek bed I finally reached was dry but entirely covered with wet fallen leaves, which disguised the rocks and crevices and made the footing treacherous. Heading downstream to the west, I soon took a tumble in a slick pothole and banged my knee on a boulder. I wasn't badly hurt but was forced to rest and to ponder my predicament should I crack a kneecap or sprain an ankle here, surrounded by acres of trail-less greenbriar and scrub.

The briar jungle finally ended at a fence and horse pasture, just as the stream gradient fell away sharply into hardwoods south and west. I walked due north through the pasture and joined a main trail. Then I headed east amid pine groves and pale prairie glades, not stopping until I reached the old cabin cellar south of Red Dog Lodge. The bare sumacs in and around it stood out from afar like huge candelabras, and the sunken stone walls made a good windbreak as I hunkered down beside them, gulped my coffee, and massaged my tender knee.

November 14

A cloudless day, warming slowly from the thirties. I went north in the eastern sector, a short ways down the trail from Deer Park Road.

This is a region of pine and oak woods interspersed by gullies and creeks. In a valley, where old pits and spoil-heaps show evidence of mining, the banks were lined with barberry and that other sign of human intrusion (because it, too, is a favorite ornamental and frequent escape), eastern red cedar (*Juniperus virginiana*). Scarlet fruits glowed in the sun-shafts and against dull earthen ridges, and a single pitch pine, still green, had collapsed across the water.

In order to follow one streamside deer trail in the direction I desired, I had to crawl on hands and knees through a short tunnel of greenbriar. I flushed so many deer along the ridges above me that they often appeared like shooting-gallery targets, three or four bursting suddenly in view—in mechanical single-file canters—before quickly dropping from sight on the other side of the hills.

I pursued them, climbing to the west, to the prairies beyond the groves—a region behind some houses where I had never walked before. These glades have recently come into pines: single trees and scattered copses, grown to heights just over my head. I used one pine as a backrest, sitting to scribble down some notes.

As I wrote these lines in my notebook, a big eight-point buck appeared in the corner of my sight. He approached me straight-on, head lowered, straining to make me out. I snorted, and he stepped within fifteen yards, then snorted himself, and bolted when I moved my arm to one side.

That deer are color-blind—as has long been believed—seems certain. I was wearing a red knit cap, with my red pack beside me, yet the buck was undeterred. He circled me through the pines and oaks, about fifty yards away, and approached me with head erect. Fascinated, I encouraged him by scraping a stick on the trunk beside me. But something else spooked him, and he snorted, turned violently, and bounded away.

A hunter could have made short work of this cocky male, who was protecting his sizeable harem and looking out for rivals.

November 16

A warm and blustery day, with variable winds and sudden showers. Donna and I hiked the middle sector, west of Red Dog Lodge.

After exploring the upper glades we climbed down to the grassy floodplain along Chimney Branch, where Donna discovered a single blue blossom of fringed gentian, closed but in good condition. Searching further, we found two more such hardy blooms on two separate plants.

There have been many days of frost this season. The low, one recent morning, was nineteen degrees, and on three successive mornings was only in the twenties. Clearly this place in the valley offers rare protection, for we found no living blossoms—gentian or otherwise—further up the valley, where in season they are prolific.

November 19

Clear and warm. I got off-trail behind the Choate Mine in an open woods of post, blackjack, and chestnut oaks. Many of the remnant oak leaves now hang in rustling clusters, as they will much of the winter, scraping loudly with each strong breeze like playing cards pinned to bike spokes.

I sat against a tree trunk and watched three deer—a doe and two yearlings—pass to one side, followed later by another big doe. Once again I wasn't noticed as a threat, though sitting in plain view with red hat and pack. The lead doe merely looked ahead, or glanced aside at the slightest angle, stopping once to listen. They all passed single file within twenty-five yards of my post. Their hooves rustled the oak leaves, and a lone cricket chirped, down among the rusty, half-bare blueberries.

When I continued I found many deer beds in the buffy patches of fescue between the trees. I saw my first hermit thrushes of the fall, a pair of them in a pine grove near a creek.

I cut northeast, diagonally through young woodlands so dense with thin oaks that the ground was ankle deep with their leaves. Far off I heard a swishing and splashing sound—like a mounted brigade crossing shallow creeks in some old time Western—and determined it was the sound of deer, alarmed and moving swiftly through the wash of brittle leaves. I stopped for five minutes, just stood where I was, and when I moved again saw a buck—who had stayed behind or circled back to check me out—leap suddenly away.

I entered a hillside stand of mountain laurel, picking my way on deer trails. From certain angles the shiny laurel leaves glared as if wet or crowned with ice. I drank coffee on the crest of a high wooded hill, viewing farm fields through branches to the north. Flocks of northern juncos scattered left and right on my return, seeming to swell and shrink in unison before landing, with an odd sort of pulsing grace.

November 23

It was bright and balmy as we walked the eastern sector, which was perfumed with wet, pitchy odors.

After yesterday's hard rain the trails in the barrens run with rivulets and are filled with reddish pine needles that raft in still pools beside rocks, like miniature logjams.

The deer continue unavoidable, even on main trails. At one point a doe and buck crossed the path ahead of us, left to right, the doe lingering to stare. The anxious buck backtracked to nudge her forward out of danger, but, in the right-hand trees further down, the rest of the herd had already decided to panic in the opposite direction, and seven does and yearlings sprinted back right to left across the trail. Our buck then had no choice but to lead his doe before us once more— right to left—and hurriedly join the others.

November 24

Donna and I attended the formal dedication of the Soldiers Delight Visitor Center. Fraser had set out his rock collection on a table in the main display room, and for the first time I got to see it. He has some nice examples of serpentinite, picrolite, mica, soapstone, chromite, and limonite.

Elsewhere, I was especially intrigued by several enlarged aerial photos of Soldiers Delight. One picture, taken in 1937, clearly showed pale bare ground over what is now the park. A second photo from 1971 showed the great encroachment of trees—dark areas that were probably mostly pines. And finally a 1984 photo showed trees so dense that dark spots cover the region, and obscure even parts of the roads.

November 27

Cold. Seventeen degrees at dawn. In the eastern end of the northwest sector I found that Fraser's volunteers have sawed many of the pines to stumps, in an effort to save the prairies. The work was recent, for dozens of cut trees lay scattered through the glades, as green as those sold at Christmas.

In the woods above one stream, common greenbriar has achieved amazing dominance, blotting the understory and forming thick curtains amid the oaks and cedars, to a height of thirty feet. There are many eastern red cedar nearby—tall, and having a neat columnar appearance, as if trimmed in topiary fashion.

The invasion of pines in this region of prairie remnants is so severe that what is pictured as an open glade on my six-year-old map, is now largely pine woods.

Above me, between patrols of windblown crows, a Cooper's hawk flew past—flapping, gliding, and flapping, then dropping down to the conifers. Later, when I rested in a piney valley, the crows got after an owl, who bolted from his cedar roost when the pressure became too much.

A gloomy woodland like this one can mean death for small birds and mammals. Like much of Dickens's London, it is a place of "dark and fearful night," at least for small wild birds.

Great horned, barred, and screech owls lurk unseen in the evergreen branches. And it's not much better in daylight, with Cooper's and sharp-shinned hawks taking up where the owls left off. Little wonder that other birds—even the smallest chickadees and kinglets—set up their own patrols, and raise a din of anger wherever they find their foes.

November 30

This was a morning of rapid weather change, beginning with sun. Donna and I hiked the eastern sector in a circuit from north to south.

Beside Red Run someone had wedged the devoured carcass of a deer—a young four-point buck—in the fork of a small oak. In this season, even from a distance, one easily picks such things out, for the trees are nearly bare. Land contours, too, are more prominent, and the visible bend and flow of little ravines and stream-cuts gives the sense of a different landscape in places we've walked many times. Tree trunks are exposed in novel ways: conspicuously gnarled old oaks, leaning and half-collapsed poplars, blotchy, serpent-skinned sycamores.

As I have sometimes felt before, there was a strangeness in the air, as of imminent violence or transformation. It always seems strongest at times of seasonal change. Today I watched its palpable clues in the odd sky and weather: a warm spring-like wind rushing from the south and west, low black rain clouds converging on a field of gray, a sudden shower of droplets, gusts turning out of the north, a breach of blue in the east. Just once, and very faintly, I thought I heard thunder far off, like a big engine shutting down.

December

Firmly Possessed by Them All

Black and Turkey Vultures

Coyote and Christmas Fern

Colossal Tree Canker

December 4

The weather—indeed, the season—seems suspended. It is not yet winter, though hardly autumn, either, for bursts of summer warmth crop up and sometimes springlike showers. Today a dusting of snow met the dawn after days of warm rain. When I left for the northwest sector it was windy and the sky clear. Then a great ridge of black clouds appeared on the horizon, and the ridge became a mountain.

I started out on the farmfield road and was soon being pelted with snow. Yet snow had been nowhere in the forecast. Big flakes came first followed by soft white pellets like laundry soap, which, driven upon the wind, completely coated my jacket.

I entered the woods by the big sycamore, seeking shelter from strong gusts. The snow became a storm. The wind abruptly shifted from northwest to east, forming crosshatched trajectories of white. A single bunch of scarlet berries—from a trodden jack-in-the-pulpit—was pinned on the ground like a broach and was soon covered with flakes. Christmas ferns were the last green forms, vivid against the pale.

It snowed madly for twenty minutes. The forest became a blur, and high winds thrashed the treetops, breaking limbs to the ground. I became whitened, as if dipped in flour, and proceeded like a figure in a glass paperweight, encased in a flake-swirled globe.

As quickly as the snow started, it stopped. The sun ap-

peared, and the sky turned icy blue. Each trunk was pow-
dered on its northwest flank. The leaves lay frosted like con-
fections; the wind moaned overhead. Birds spoke up—downies, chickadees, titmice—amazed, it seemed, by the changes.

I walked a good ways through this wonderland, and when
the snow began to melt, came uphill toward a farm field. Wet
leaves glared, weed stalks twinkled like crystal, pine boughs
glistened and winked. Behind me, down in the wooded valley,
the wind roared through the canopy like a train, then burst
onto the high ground, flailing each twig and bush. There was
some danger in it. Shrieking gusts felled branches around me
while old oaks creaked and tilted. I avoided the trees in the
last half mile, watched snow-devils twist in the fields, and was
blown off balance in the lot by my car, where the wind whistled with Hollywood drama, the sky darkened once more,
and a snow squall fogged the air.

December 6

Overcast and cold. I worked down to the southern end of
the northwest sector, to the beaver cove of Locust Run. It has
disappeared entirely. The stream is there, of course, gurgling
west in its eroded bed. But all else is dry.

I walked a while and sat on a rock where the stream finally
reaches the lake. I pondered the drastic change before me—
from record high water last May, to record reduction now. My
view was of a clearly man-made landscape, rather ugly now,
where six months before it was gorgeous. A belted kingfisher
flew over, and two pileated woodpeckers, but their impact
was somehow diminished.

Hiking back on the sandy lake bed, I noticed foxlike tracks

running straight for forty yards before vanishing in the leaves. I measured the paw prints at 2½ inches long, and the stride—in this case probably a trot—at 12 inches. The red fox has an average trotting stride of 11 inches, and 1¾ inch paw prints. Of course, there are many dogs about, but they don't walk far in straight lines. So I couldn't help thinking about coyotes. Their trotting stride runs 13 inches, but their paw prints are 2½, the same as these in the lake bed. I had always wondered about that beaver of last winter, whose gnawed pelt I had found not a hundred yards from this spot. Could a red fox really have handled him, even in surprise attack? Or had it been something larger?

The idea of coyotes around Soldiers Delight is not at all far-fetched. They and their pups have been spotted in northern Baltimore County and as near as Sparks and Glyndon. Carcasses, too, have been found. I learned all this recently from Peter Jayne at the Maryland DNR. Never before known in the East, even in days of old, coyotes have spread from their strongholds in the West and are now invading Maryland. All of Pennsylvania's counties report coyotes as do all but one in western and northern Maryland. Coyotes drive out foxes, which could partly explain the red fox invasion in the densest parts of our suburbs.

Even bobcats are expanding. They've been found in Carroll County—our neighbor to the west—and also in Anne Arundel, by the Chesapeake Bay, though the latter were probably hunting club imports.

About cougars. There are none. Not in Maryland, nor anywhere in the East except Florida, which shelters a separate race. There are certainly none at Soldiers Delight, nor in Randallstown, where one or two were "reported" last year just two blocks from our home. And there haven't been any in the East since the last one was shot for bounty, in the New York Adirondacks, in the winter of 1890.

I wish I could say it weren't so. But a hundred years of hunting and tracking don't lie, nor does the extensive field research carried out by expert biologists, beginning around 1980, in every likely habitat. The research intent was to confirm breeding, but even unmated individuals proved elusive. A single adult animal was found near the Great Smokies, and that was a western cougar, released by, or escaped from, humans.

There was some excitement in the 1970s. One cougar was killed, and another was captured, in an eastern West Virginia county. But authorities grew suspicious at how easily the live one was caught. It came up and got real friendly when someone played country music. Not quite your wild-bred beastie. Both were later revealed to be imports from the West. As far as I know, the live one couldn't run a stereo system, but perhaps that is next.

December 8

Balmy after days of cold. I looked for more tracks this morning, in the bed of Liberty Lake, but without success.

Paw prints, in the case of animals like coyotes, are not the best proof of their presence; besides being easily confused with those of dogs, they expand in wet soil and are altered by age, rain, and thawing. And, if a lot is at stake, paw prints can easily be faked. Take, for example, cougars. One local gentleman, who insists they exist at Soldiers Delight, has told me he has plaster casts of their paw prints. Once again, pet or zoo cougars—or even stuffed trophies—can easily be used to make prints. As further "evidence" of their likely presence, he cites the abundance of white-tailed deer, once the big cat's chief prey; by that criterion—with deer at nuisance levels even in city parks—there are cougars in Baltimore and Washington.

Yet some people still insist. There are cougars at Soldiers Delight. Alligators in New York. Monsters in Chesapeake Bay. Because people *want* them to be there. They want wild beasties, want to think they are just down the road, or lurking in their yard or woodlot. A panther, a Bigfoot, a dragon. Folks are, much like our primitive forebears, longing for spirits of the woodlands, wishing for untamed wonders, looking for mystery and myth.

But, balancing the human desire for mythic animal presence, must be the need for rational truth. Reason and reality tell us we've killed the awesome beasts to satisfy our blood lust. We have also cut down their homes—at least in much of the East—to make way for our own lives of comfort. So our rational selves should tell us that we can't have it both ways. You want poodles, and Penney's, and Popeye's Fried Chicken? Then you don't get imposing beasties, in any place but the zoo.

But we are greedy and foolish little monkeys. We want what we've already wasted; we deny what is all too clear. Some of us even plant grass round the porch, ritually spray it each season, and insist that we've then seen mountain lions between the swing-set and the grill.

The odd thing is that they're out there. If not quite in the yard, at least in a place nearby—a place like Soldiers Delight. Untamed, mysterious creatures. I'm quite willing to admit it. In fact, I must insist. They're just not big and ferocious. They don't growl and bellow. But find me a long-tailed salamander, or a lurking fence lizard. Seek out a queen snake or copperhead. And I'll show you a thing untamed, show you mystery and myth. Search for those things and more, and I'll show you—in both the questing and the object of the quest—a kind of subtle beauty that runs only through our dreams.

December 11

I walked west from the overlook on a day that started cold. The hoarfrost had settled like granulated sugar on clumps of serpentine chickweed. Beside Chimney Branch it rimed the dormant grasses and edged the trail with white. It was very still in the valley. A smokelike mist rose from the greenbriar thickets, as if they were on fire.

There was a freshness about the glades this morning. Astringent odors of pine, sun steeling the frost-melt under a blue porcelain sky, the scouring wash and gurgle of the recently risen stream—all of it made me feel cleansed and alert.

On the hillsides to the north, the gnarled aspect of the bare oaks is prominent. Their stances are stiff and scarecrowish, their bent limbs jutting at their sides, trunks scaly with pale bark and lichens, bases ill-dressed in sprouted twigs and ragged skirts of leaves.

I moved through the wet delta, observed the papery corpses of fringed gentians standing rigid here and there—their seed pods wrapped like tamales—then climbed back north and east through the prairies and oak woodlands. I stopped below the Hanging Hill and let my attention wander. The valley lay misted below me in the cold light, the crows sounded off from each hill, and truck gears ground in the distance.

December 15

Today's walk was mostly about wind-song. In the bright chill of the eastern sector, the pine boughs shook high above. Their soft, rhythmic swooshing sounded like waves on a distant beach.

In the hardwoods along Red Run it was different: open violence in the bare crowns, the odd trunk rubbing another, creaking like a rusty gate. Moments of sunny stillness were blotted by clouds, loud gusts, and the wooden-bead clatter of twigs. Donna picked sprouted acorns from the frozen leafy trails.

December 17

I hiked the northwest sector, near Liberty Lake. The reservoir now is fifteen feet below its springtime level.

The watershed fire road, and indeed the brown forest floor, are for long distances littered with the flat pale seeds of tulip-trees, whose flowerlike seed pods have dispersed this drab confetti of fruits.

My most interesting find was a tree canker, twenty feet up on the trunk of a fifty foot oak. Cankers are deformities caused by fungi, whose mycelium attack the tree's bark and cambial layers. Most cankers are fairly small. This one was shockingly huge, about five feet wide, four feet high, and three feet thick, and shaped like a great neck goiter, or the engorged throat sac of a breeding prairie chicken. Its surface was of deeply furrowed bark, much like that of the main trunk, and only a small gap in back now kept it from encircling the tree. Most tree cankers kill, scar, or deform the bark that contains them, but this one seems to have grown blandly within it—perhaps since the tree was a sapling—making its monstrous enlargement all the more strange, for the deep furrows of this oak bark were cleanly intact on the outside of the bulge.

December 20

I went up to the eastern end of the northwest sector, making one more search for the elusive table mountain pine.

The Virginia pines that were cut this fall have mostly been chipped and shredded into tidy piles on the hillsides. In one woodland I found an oak leaf oddly fastened with a pair of oak apple galls, and nearby some bright green lichens had banded the bases of pine trees as if neatly applied with a paintbrush.

In a high glade I examined three or four vertebrae from the neck of a white-tailed deer. One detached vertebral disk was of lima bean color and shape. But what soon caught my eye was a conifer glowing yellow in the distant pines. I had to descend a gully and break through greenbriar to reach it. It stood perhaps forty feet tall, on a steep slope, surrounded by Virginia pine. Could this be a table mountain pine?

Its trunk was woven with briars and impossible to scale. The chartreuse branchlets—far out of reach—I looked at through binoculars, but important details were obscured. I finally found both a branchlet and cone in the litter near the base of the tree. Needles were bundled in threes, longer than those of scrub pine, and the cone scales were tipped with prickles. Though the needles of mountain pine sometimes appear in threes, they are usually in twos, and the cone scales are spiked, not prickled. I was forced to admit this was pitch pine, a frail or diseased individual—perhaps affected by drought—whose needles had faded to this sulphurous hue and caused it to so stand out.

December 22

Sunrise on the Hanging Hill, on the shortest day of the year. I determined to do a Christmas Bird Count, in all three sectors of Soldiers Delight. I walked south from the hill, with the sky pinking to my left—first a pale, fanlike glow, then ascending bars of carmine, yellow green, orange, with a smogline above the trees. The full moon, bruised with gray, was setting in the star-pocked west.

It was quiet in the middle sector, and cold. Once a cardinal caroled, then gave up, to be succeeded by a Carolina wren. Otherwise only crows called, or passed in thin trains overhead with the odd grackle outrider. The wind rose. Metal beat against metal in the power-line pylons above, broken brackets clanging like loosely hung pots. I came back with under ten species.

In the east I did better, listing fifteen more species, including hermit thrush and swamp sparrow. Chickadees, titmice, and kinglets, skulking in stunted pines, came out to stare or to scold me as I sat cross-legged in a glade.

The northwest sector was richest, and I got there in the afternoon. A winter wren, by the Pines Branch falls, was perhaps the count's best bird. There was an eastern bluebird by a field, a flock of cedar waxwings, and a glimpse of a sharp-shinned hawk. The finest time came late in the day, when I rested in an open thicket, above a creek and a farm field. The sky was utterly cloudless—a deep, clean cerulean—and the gray branches of maples stood out sharply against it. A breeze shifted the weed stalks. I settled back on my elbows while a red-tailed hawk dove past on the wind, chestnut shoulders aglow, weightless form thrusting swiftly among the gray and blue.

December 27

I started in the eastern sector on a freezing bright morning, feeling sleepy until I reached the wet spot east of the main trail junction. Then my eyes and brain began to focus cleanly together, and I slipped into that pleasurable thrall that I have come to know so well. I knew this trail a year ago, better than any others. The place is still the same, but I am utterly changed. I feel woven into a fabric, linked to new threads of knowledge drawn from all parts of Soldiers Delight, so that anywhere in its boundaries now, I carry the whole cloth with me—seem to wear it like a cloak.

By the eagle tree I found deer bones, cleanly chewed, and boulder lichens frosted the nearby trunk with greenish dog-eared patches. I made my way to the old oak, roundabout, from the farm fields to the east. Turkey vultures tilted, and were joined by black vultures, too. I leaned against the tree and realized something was up. More blacks appeared—first three, then two, and finally a group of six—while the turkey vultures descended, and several landed in a tree.

I waited and watched where one came down. Then I left the tree and crossed the fields to the place they seemed to be gathering. When I crested the last rise a band of twelve black vultures—more than any I'd seen in the area—rose and retreated to a nearby perch. I could now smell the carcass, and found it on the edge of the woods—an unlucky seven-point buck that lay mostly devoured, in the brush. The hind- and fore-quarters were intact, the shoulders and neck looked strong, so I guessed this buck was wounded by a poacher and staggered here to die. Overabundant or not, deer like this one are graceful, and I didn't like seeing him dead. Still, scavengers have to eat, and judging from the horde of buzzards this was quite a windfall for many.

I could only imagine the pecking-order fierceness. Eighteen vultures of both species lurked beside their meal, another dozen were aloft, and three or four more seemed to trail me back—hovering low or perching—for half a mile toward my car. Perhaps their status is as lookouts, reporting back to the others. In any case, the pecking-order plot thickened. A wedge of ten black vultures—obviously late arrivals—showed up in the west when I reached the glades, and slanted toward the farm fields. This was clearly a major event, and there was bound to be some conflict. The concept of the "peaceable kingdom" never counts on overcrowding.

December 29

At the end of our cold walk in the eastern sector today, near the Choate Mine, Donna and I came upon Fraser Bishop and two companions. These were Pat Milner and her husband, collecting mineral samples from the scattered spoils near the mine entrance. Pat works for the U.S. Department of Agriculture in Beltsville, Maryland. She and her colleagues are just now beginning an experiment to see if native plant-root fungi have the ability to take up toxic minerals, such as nickel and chromium, from the soil in which they are found. If some fungal species do achieve this uptake, they could be massively reproduced and used to inoculate soil areas of high mineral toxicity, like dump sites, thus cleansing them gradually in a process of "green mining."

Soil, plants, and fungi all figure into the equation. Serpentine soil and the plants growing in it will be brought back to Pat's lab, placed in pots, and left alone for three or four months. Fungal cultures that have by then developed on the plant roots will be collected and tested for unusually high levels of nickel or chromium. Though these root-specific fungi are the same species that grow on plant roots elsewhere, it is hoped that, over eons amid serpentine soil, a special fungal "eco-type" has evolved with unique antitoxic mechanisms, such as retaining mineral ions within the fungal cells.

At this point it is all theory, and may not work as imagined. If the fungi actively block plant-root uptake of the minerals, they clearly have no site-cleansing use. And likewise, if the fungi simply ignore the toxins and leave the plants to their own coping devices, they are equally useless. For large-scale toxic cleansing there must be evidence of toxic uptake, not merely passive resistance.

Still, it's an imaginative concept, an example of how science views complexly the great complexity of nature and strives to profit by that interlacing vision.

December 31

Clear and cold in late afternoon. Park the car north of Ward's Chapel Road. Descend through the yellow-green glade pines, to the gurgling stem of Mill Run. Hear the leafy tred of deer moving uphill in the trees. Watch the fluff tails bob away. Dodge the frozen puddles in the road, their white ice swirled with brown. Find a pheasant tail-feather; stick it in your cap, like you did when ten years old. Skirt the old pasture and apple trees, the dun and olive meadow streaked with long bars of light. Hear chickadees twitter with alarm and fly up into the cedars. Pass the barren chestnuts—their husks scattered on the trail like tiny, listless hedgehogs—toward the quiet, frozen fish pond. The ice with hoary tattoos, the cattails bare and buff, the tulip-trees still set with florets and stretching above the bank.

A hornet nest, from afar, looks like a gray perching owl, the green pines clustered around it, against the lighter browns. The sun dips through trees to the west, over the Mill Run valley. Walk that way, through the woods and down the slope. Cross the stream, the woodlands strangely silent. A Cooper's hawk glides low, perches, looks for prey, then glides up over the hill, neatly explaining the silence. Ask and ye shall be told—such rapport no longer surprising. Climb to the fields, the sun now dropping swiftly, the horizon a burnished shelf supporting a bright copper plate.

The big sycamore leans, feeling its age, black against the sky. Come up from the east, to the springhouse foundations, where the black snake once fled. Only black tires here now, round castles where the herp princes sleep. Feel the rough mossy bark of the massive time machine. Now the little ritual, the one played out all year. Drop the bright red day pack—once traveling home to a serpent, loose conveyance for the flotsam of discovery. Remove the squat thermos, pour out the steaming brew, with the flourish demanded by its spout. Take a hot, bitter-sweet gulp.

The sun sinks over the distant lake, somewhere beyond the hill. Wrens call, and a single robin chortles. Wait for some other sign, some herald of the year's closing circle. It is never what you expect.

Hear the footfalls, distinctly human, behind and to the right. He approaches. Sit perfectly still. A bow-hunter, looking for deer, arrow casually ready, passing a few yards away. Call out? Or be still, and test the auspicious aura? Be still, the tree enfolds you. Red pack beside you, red cap on your head, yet the hunter does not notice and walks out into the field. Watch him as he meets the farm road and tramps off into the dusk. Have you somehow merged with the forest, gone invisible, become a canker on a tree? Hardly. The song sparrow knows and scolds you from a bush, as do titmice and chickadees. They make it plain, near night-roost time, that you are an unwelcome troll.

Up now. Heading home, with the light nearly gone, the day and year as well. A red wash left in the west. Things are as they should be, as they have been here, for too many years to count. It is their place in the end, always has been, firmly possessed by them all, the wild things of Soldiers Delight.

Appendix

Bibliography

Index

Appendix

The scientific names of flora and fauna mentioned in the text are listed below.

Flora

amanita, panther (*Amanita velatipes*)
anemone, rue *(Anemonella)*
anemone, wood (*Anemone*)
apple, domestic (*Pyrus malus*)
arbutus, trailing (*Epigaea repens*)
aspen (*Populus*)
   quaking (*P. tremuloides*)
   big-toothed (*P. grandidentata*)
aster (*Aster*)
   New York (*A. novae-belgii*)
   serpentine (*A. depauperatus*)
   small white (*A. vimineus*)
barberry, European (*Berberis vulgaris*)
bergamot, wild (*Monarda fistulosa*)
bindweed, white-flowered (*Convolvulus arvensis*)
birch, river (*Betula nigra*)
bittersweet, American (*Celastris scandens*)
blackberry (*Rubus* species)
black-eyed Susan (*Rudbeckia hirta*)
blazing-star, (*Liatris*)
   grass-leaved *(L. graminifolia)*
   dense *(L. spicata)*

bloodroot (*Sanguinaria canadensis*)
bluestem (*Andropogon*)
  big (*A. gerardi*)
  little (*A. scoparius*)
bluet (*Houstonia caerulea*)
boneset (*Eupatorium perfoliatum*)
boxelder (*Acer negundo*)
bristlegrass (green foxtail) (*Seteria viridis*)
broom moss (*Dicranum* species)
broomsage (broomsedge) (*Andropogon virginicus*)
broomsedge (broomsage) (*Andropogon virginicus*)
bulrush (*Scirpus* species)
bush-clover (*Lespedeza* species)
cardinal flower (*Lobelia cardinalis*)
cattail, common (*Typha latifolia*)
cedar, eastern red (*Juniperus virginiana*)
chanterelle waxy cap (*Hygrophorus cantharellus*)
cherry (*Prunus*)
  black (*P. serotina*)
  eastern dwarf (*P. susquehanae*)
  sour (*P. cerasus*)
chestnut (*Castanea*)
  American (*C. dentata*)
  Chinese (*C. mollissima*)
chickweed, serpentine (hairy field) (*Cerastium arvense var. villosum*)
chicory (*Cichorium intybus*)
chinkapin, Allegheny (*Castanea pumila*)
Christmas fern (*Polystichum acrostichoides*)
cinquefoil, common (dwarf) (*Potentilla canadensis*)
cinquefoil, dwarf (common) (*Potentilla canadensis*)
clammy calocera (*Calocera viscosa*)
cord moss (*Funaria* species)
creeper, Virginia (*Parthenocissus quinquefolia*)
daisy (family *Compositae*)
dayflower, Asiatic (*Commelina communis*)
deerberry (*Vaccinium stamineum*)

deptford pink (*Dianthus armeria*)
dogwood, flowering (*Cornus florida*)
false Solomon's-seal (*Smilacina* species)
fameflower (*Talinum teretifolium*)
fescue grass (*Festuca* species)
fimbry, annual (*Fimbristylis annua*)
flax, grooved yellow (*Linum sulcatum*)
foxtail, green (bristlegrass) (*Setaria viridis*)
gamagrass, eastern (*Tripsacum dactyloides*)
gentian, fringed (*Gentianopsis crinita*)
gerardia (*Agalinas*)
   purple (*A. purpurea*)
   sandplain (*A. acuta*)
   slender (*A. tenuifolia*)
   A. obtusifolia
   A. fasciculata
gill-over-the-ground (*Glechoma hederacea*)
goldenrod (*Solidago*)
   early (*S. juncea*)
   gray (*S. nemoralis*)
   lance-leaved (*S. graminifolia*)
grape, wild (*Vitis* species)
greenbriar (*Smilax*)
   common (*S. rotundifolia*)
   glaucous (*S. glauca*)
ground pine, running (*Lycopodium complanatum*)
gum, black (black tupelo) (*Nyssa sylvatica*)
gum, black tupelo (black) (*Nyssa sylvatica*)
hairgrass, tufted (*Deschampsia caespitosa*)
hay-scented fern (*Dennstaedtia punctilobula*)
heal-all (*Prunella vulgaris*)
hemlock, eastern (*Tsuga canadensis*)
hepatica, round-lobed (*Hepatica americana*)
hickory (*Carya*)
   bitternut (*C. cordiformis*)
   mockernut (*C. tomentosa*)

shagbark (*C. ovata*)
holy (vanilla) grass (*Hierochloe odorata*)
horse nettle (*Solanum carolinense*)
horsetail (*Equisetum*)
huckleberry, black (*Gaylussacia baccata*)
Indian grass (*Sorghastrum nutans*)
ironweed, New York (*Vernonia noveboracensis*)
ivy, poison (*Rhus radicans*)
jack-in-the-pulpit (*Arisaema tryphyllum*)
jewelweed (touch-me-not) (*Impatiens capensis*)
joe-pye weed (*Eupatorium* species)
knotweed, slender (*Polygonum tenue*)
ladies' tresses, slender (*Spirathes gracilis*)
laurel, mountain (*Kalmia latifolia*)
lichen, boulder (*Parmelia* species)
lichen (*Cladonia*)
    British soldiers (red crest) (*C. cristatella*)
    reindeer (*C.* species)
lobelia, great (*Lobelia siphilitica*)
locust, black (*Robinia pseudo-acacia*)
maple (*Acer*)
    Norway (*A. platanoides*)
    red (*A. rubrum*)
milkweed (*Asclepias*)
    common (*A. syriaca*)
    green (*A. viridiflora*)
    whorled (*A. verticillata*)
milkwort, whorled (*Polygala verticillata*)
monkey-flower, square-stemmed (*Mimulus ringens*)
mint (family *Labiatae*)
mocassin flower (pink lady's slipper) (*Cypripedium acaule*)
moss phlox (moss-pink) (*Phlox subulata*)
moss-pink (moss phlox) (*Phlox subulata*)
mullein, common (*Verbascum thapsus*)
mushroom, amanita (*Amanita* species)
oak (*Quercus*)

bear (scrub) (*Q. ilicifolia*)
blackjack (*Q. marilandica*)
chestnut (*Q. prinus*)
northern red (*Q. rubra*)
post (*Q. stellata*)
scrub (bear) (*Q. ilicifolia*)
olive, autumn (oleaster) (*Elaeagnus umbella*)
orchard grass (*Dactylis glomerata*)
orchis, showy (*Orchis spectablis*)
partridge-pea, large-flowered (*Cassia fasciculata*)
path rush (*Juncus tenuis*)
pea, everlasting (*Lathyrus latifolius*)
peat moss (*Sphagnum palustre*)
peat moss (*Sphagnum capillaceum*)
persimmon (*Dyospyros virginia*)
pine (*Pinus*)
   mountain (table mountain) (*P. pungens*)
   pitch (*P. rigida*)
   table mountain (mountain) (*P. pungens*)
   Virginia (scrub pine) (*P. virginiana*)
pink lady's slipper (mocassin flower) (*Cypripedium acaule*)
pipsissewa (*Chimaphila umbellata*)
plantain, downy rattlesnake (*Goodyera pubescens*)
pokeweed (*Phytolacca americana*)
polypore, milk-white toothed (*Irpex lacteus*)
polypore mushroom (family Polyporaceae)
poverty grass (three-awn) (*Aristida dichotoma*)
prairie willow, dwarf (*Salix humilis* var. *microphylla*)
puffball, gem-studded (*Lycoperdon perlatum*)
pussytoes, plantain-leaved (*Antennaria plantaginifolia*)
purpletop (*Tridens flavus*)
pyxie cup (goblet lichen) (*Cladonia pyxidata*)
Queen Anne's lace (*Daucus carota*)
ragwort, small's (*Senecio anonymous*)
rattlebox (*Crotalaria sagittalis*)
redbud, eastern (*Cercis canadensis*)

rock cress, lyre-leaved (*Arabis lyrata*)
rose (*Rosa*)
    Carolina (pasture rose) (*R. carolina*)
    multiflora (*R. multiflora*)
    pasture rose (Carolina) (*R. carolina*)
rose-pink (*Sabatia angularis*)
russula, short-stalked white (*Russula brevipes*)
sassafras (*Sassafras albidum*)
saxifrage, early (*Saxifraga virginiensis*)
sedge, umbrella (*Cyperus* species)
sensitive fern (*Onoclea sensibilis*)
serpentine (hairy field) chickweed (*Cerastium arvense* var. *villosum*)
shadbush (*Amelanchier arborea*)
skunk cabbage (*Symplocarpus foetidus*)
slender blue-eyed grass (*Sisyrinchium mucronatum*)
smartweed (*Polygonum* species)
snakeroot, white (*Eupatorium rugosum*)
spicebush, common (*Lindera benzoin*)
spiderwort (*Tradescantia virginiana*)
spikerush (*Eleocharis* species)
split gill, common (*Schizophyllum commune*)
spring-beauty (*Claytonia virginica*)
sumac, staghorn (*Rhus typhina*)
sundrop (*Oenothera* species)
sycamore, American (*Platanus occidentalis*)
three-awn (poverty grass) (*Aristida dichotoma*)
    purplish (*A. purpurascens*)
tick-trefoil (*Desmodium*)
   large-bracted (*D. cuspidatum*)
   linear-leaved (*D. lineatum*)
   naked-flowered (*D. nudiflorum*)
   rigid (*D. rigidum*)
   small-leaved (*D. ciliare*)
toothwort, slender (*Dentaria heterophylla*)
tree club moss (*Lycopodium obscurum*)
tulip-tree (yellow poplar) (*Liriodendron tulipifera*)

vanilla (holy) grass (*Hierochloe odorata*)
viburnum, maple-leaf (*Viburnum acerifolium*)
violet (*Viola*)
   arrow-leaved (*V. sagittata*)
   birdfoot (*V. pedata*)
   common blue (*V. papilionacea*)
   ovate-leaved (*V. fimbriatula*)
   yellow (*V. rotundifolia*)
walnut, black (*Juglans nigra*)
water moss, common (*Fontinalis* species)
white cushion moss (*Leucobryum glaucum*)
wineberry (*Rubus phoenicolasius*)
witch-hazel (*Hammamelis virginiana*)
wintergreen, spotted (*Chimaphila maculata*)

Fauna

acadian flycatcher (*Empidonax virescens*)
American crow (*Corus brachyrhynchos*)
American goldfinch (*Carduelis tristis*)
American redstart (*Setophaga ruticilla*)
American robin (*Turdus migratorius*)
American toad (*Bufo americanus*)
American woodcock (*Scolopax minor*)
annual cicada (dogday harvestfly) (*Tibicen canicularis*)
bald eagle (*Haliaeetus leucocephalus*)
barred owl (*Strix varia*)
beaver (*Castor canadensis*)
belted kingfisher (*Ceryle alcyon*)
black-and-white warbler (*Mniotilta varia*)
black bear (*Ursus americanus*)
black-billed cuckoo (*Coccyzus erythropthalmus*)
blacknose dace (*Rhinichthys atratulus*)
black rat snake (*Elaphe obsoleta obsoleta*)
black-throated blue warbler (*Dendroica caerulescens*)
black-throated green warbler (*Dendroica virens*)

black vulture (*Coragyps atratus*)
black-winged damselfly (*Calopteryx maculata*)
bluegill (*Lepomis macrochirus*)
blue-gray gnatcatcher (*Polioptila caerulea*)
blue jay (*Cyanocitta cristata*)
blue-winged warbler (*Vermivora pinus*)
bobcat (*Lynx rufus*)
bobolink (*Dolichonyx oryzivorus*)
broad-winged hawk (*Buteo platypterus*)
brown-headed cowbird (*Molothrus ater*)
buckeye (*Junonia coenia*)
caddisfly (order Trichoptera)
Canada goose (*Branta canadensis*)
Carolina chickadee (*Parus carolinensis*)
Carolina wren (*Thryothorus ludovicianus*)
carp (*Cyprinus carpio*)
carrion beetle (*Silpha* species)
cedar waxwing (*Bombycilla cedrorum*)
chestnut-sided warbler (*Dendroica pensylvanica*)
chimney swift (*Chaetura pelagica*)
chuck-will's-widow (*Caprimulgus carolinensis*)
common blue (*Celastrina argiolus*)
common grackle (*Quiscalus quiscula*)
common loon (*Gavia immer*)
common merganser (*Mergus merganser*)
common wood nymph (*Cercyonis pegala*)
common yellowthroat (*Geothlypis trichas*)
Cooper's hawk (*Accipiter cooperii*)
coral hairstreak (*Harkenclenus titus*)
cougar (*Felis concolor*)
coyote (*Canis latrans*)
darkling beetle (*Polypleurus perforatus*)
deer tick (*Ixodes dammini*)
dobsonfly (*Corydalus* species)
dogday harvestfly (annual cicada) (*Tibicen canicularis*)
downy woodpecker (*Picoides pubescens*)

dragonfly (order Odonata)
earthworm (Oligochaeta)
eastern bluebird (*Sialia sialis*)
eastern blue darner (*Aeshna verticalis*)
eastern box turtle (*Terrapene carolina carolina*)
eastern cottontail (*Sylvilagus floridanus*)
eastern crayfish (*Cambarus bartoni*)
eastern garter snake (*Thamnophis sirtalis sirtalis*)
eastern gray squirrel (*Sciurus carolinensis*)
eastern hog-nosed snake (*Heterodon platyrhinos*)
eastern phoebe (*Sayornis phoebe*)
eastern screech owl (*Otus asio*)
Edwards hairstreak (*Satyrium edwardsii*)
European starling (*Sturnus vulgaris*)
fence lizard (*Sceloporus undulatus*)
field cricket (*Gryllus* species)
field sparrow (*Spizella pusilla*)
fox sparrow (*Passerella iliaca*)
funnel weaver spider (family Agelenidae)
gall wasp (family Cynipinae)
garden slug (sub-class Pulmonata)
golden-crowned kinglet (*Regulus satrapa*)
golden eagle (*Aquila chrysaetos*)
golden-winged warbler (*Vermivora chrysoptera*)
gray catbird (*Dumetella carolinensis*)
great blue heron (*Ardea herodias*)
great horned owl (*Bubo virginianus*)
great spangled fritillary (*Speyeria cybele*)
green-backed heron (*Butorides striatus*)
green tiger beetle (*Cinindela* species)
gypsy moth (*Porthetria dispar*)
hermit thrush (*Catharus guttatus*)
honeybee (*Apis mellifera*)
hooded merganser (*Lophodytes cucullatus*)
hooded warbler (*Wilsonia citrina*)
house finch (*Carpodacus mexicanus*)

indigo bunting (*Passerina cyanea*)

Japanese beetle (*Popillia japonica*)

juvenal's dusky-wing (*Erynnis juvenalis*)

Kentucky warbler (*Oporornis formosus*)

largemouth bass (*Micropterus salmoides*)

little wood satyr (*Euptychia cymela*)

locust leaf miner (*Xenochalepus dorsalis*)

long-tailed salamander (*Eurycea longicauda longicauda*)

Louisiana waterthrush (*Seiurus motacilla*)

magnolia warbler (*Dendroica magnolia*)

mallard (*Anas platyrhynchos*)

mayfly (order Ephemeroptera)

monarch (*Danaus plexippus*)

mottled sculpin (*Cottus bairdi*)

mound-building ant (subfamily Formicinae)

narrow-winged damselfly (family Coenagrionidae)

northern bobwhite (*Colinus virginianus*)

northern caddisfly (family Limnephilidae)

northern cardinal (*Cardinalis cardinalis*)

northern copperhead (*Agkistrodon contortrix*)

northern dusky salamander (*Desmognathus fuscus fuscus*)

northern flicker (*Colaptes auratus*)

northern harrier (*Circus cyaneus*)

northern junco (*Junco hyemalis*)

northern oriole (Baltimore oriole) (*Icterus galbula*)

northern parula warbler (*Parula americana*)

northern two-lined salamander (*Eurycea bislineata bislineata*)

northern waterthrush (*Seiurus noveboracensis*)

orb-weaver spider (*Micrathena* species)

osprey (*Pandion haliaetus*)

ovenbird (*Seiurus aurocapillus*)

painted lady (*Vanessa cardui*)

painted lichen moth (*Hypoprepia fucosa*)

palm warbler (*Dendroica palmarum*)

pearly crescent (*Phyciodes tharus*)

periodical cicada (*Magicicada* species)

pileated woodpecker (*Dryocopus pileatus*)
pine warbler (*Dendroica pinus*)
prairie warbler (*Dendroica discolor*)
purple finch (*Carpodacus purpureus*)
queen snake (*Natrix septemvittata*)
raccoon (*Procyon lotor*)
red-backed salamander (*Plethodon cinerus cinerus*)
red-bellied woodpecker (*Melanerpes carolinus*)
red-breasted nuthatch (*Sitta canadensis*)
red crossbill (*Loxia curvirostra*)
red-eyed vireo (*Vireo olivaceus*)
red fox (*Vulpes fulva*)
red-shouldered hawk (*Buteo lineatus*)
red-spotted purple (*Basilarchia astyanax*)
red-tailed hawk (*Buteo jamaicensis*)
red-throated loon (*Gavia stellata*)
ring-billed gull (*Larus delawarensis*)
ring-necked pheasant (*Phasianus colchicus*)
rosyside dace (*Clinostomus funduloides*)
ruby-crowned kinglet (*Regulus calendula*)
rufous-sided towhee (*Pipilio erythrophthalmus*)
scarlet tanager (*Piranga olivacea*)
sharp-shinned hawk (*Accipiter striatus*)
silver-spotted skipper (*Epargyreus clarus*)
smallmouth bass (*Micropterus dolomieu*)
snapping turtle (*Chelydra serpentina*)
solitary sandpiper (*Tringa solitaria*)
solitary vireo (*Vireo solitarius*)
song sparrow (*Melospiza melodia*)
sooty-wing (*Pholisora catullus*)
southern leopard frog (*Rana utricularia*)
sowbug (*Porcellio* species)
spicebush swallowtail (*Papilio troilus*)
springtail (*Achorutes nivicolus*)
stonefly (order Plecoptera)
striped bass/rockfish (*Morone saxatilis*)

Swainson's thrush (*Catharus ustulatus*)
swamp sparrow (*Melospiza georgiana*)
tiger swallowtail (*Papilio glaucus*)
tree swallow (*Tachycineta bicolor*)
tufted titmouse (*Parus bicolor*)
water strider (*Gerris marginatus*)
whip-poor-will (*Caprimulgus vociferus*)
white-breasted nuthatch (*Sitta carolinensis*)
white-eyed vireo (*Vireo griseus*)
white-tailed deer (*Odocoileus virginianus*)
white-throated sparrow (*Zonotrichia albicollis*)
whirligig beetle (family Gyrinidae)
wild turkey (*Meleagris gallopavo*)
winter wren (*Troglodytes troglodytes*)
woodchuck (*Marmota monax*)
wood duck (*Aix sponsa*)
wood frog (*Rana sylvatica*)
wood tick (*Dermacentor andersoni*)
worm-eating warbler (*Helmitheros vermivorus*)
yellow-billed cuckoo (*Coccyzus americanus*)
yellow-breasted chat (*Icteria virens*)
yellow-rumped warbler (*Dendroica coronata*)
yellow-throated vireo (*Vireo flavifrons*)

Bibliography

Borror, Donald J., and Richard E. White. *A Field Guide to the Insects.* Boston: Houghton Mifflin, 1970.

Brockman, C. Frank. *Trees of North America.* New York: Western Publishing Company, 1968.

Brooks, Robert R. *Serpentine and Its Vegetation: A Multi-Disciplinary Approach.* Portland, Oreg.: Dioscorides Press, 1987.

Brown, Melvin L., and Russell G. Brown. *Herbaceous Plants of Maryland.* Baltimore: Port City Press, Inc., 1984.

Bulletin of the Maryland Natural Heritage Program. Maryland Department of Natural Resources; Forest, Park, and Wildlife Service, 1990.

Burt, William H., and Richard P. Grossenheider. *A Field Guide to the Mammals.* Boston: Houghton Mifflin, 1952.

Chesterman, Charles W. *The Audubon Society Field Guide to North American Rocks and Minerals.* New York: Alfred A. Knopf, Inc., 1978.

Clark, William Bullock. *Report on the Physical Features of Maryland; Maryland Geological Survey.* Baltimore, Md.: Johns Hopkins University Press, 1906.

Conant, Roger. *A Field Guide to Reptiles and Amphibians.* Boston: Houghton Mifflin, 1958.

Covell, Charles V. Jr. *A Field Guide to the Moths of Eastern North America.* Boston: Houghton Mifflin, 1984.

Dana, Edward S. *A Textbook of Mineralogy.* New York: John Wiley & Sons, 1922.

Dann, Kevin T. *Traces on the Appalachians.* New Brunswick, N.J.: Rutgers University Press, 1988.

Field Guide to the Birds of North America. Washington, D.C.: National Geographic Society, 1983.

Fisher, Alan. *Country Walks Near Baltimore.* Appalachian Mountain Club, 1981.

Gleason, Henry A. *The New Britton and Brown Illustrated Flora of the Northeast United States and Adjacent Canada.* New York: Hafner Press, 1974.

Hamilton, W. R., A. R. Woolley, and A. C. Bishop. *A Guide to Minerals, Rocks, and Fossils.* New York: Hamlyn Publishing Group Limited, 1974.

Harlow, William M. *Trees of the Eastern and Central United States and Canada.* New York: Dover Publications, Inc., 1957.

Herrera, Wilson. "Ore Washing in Soldiers Delight". *History Trails.* Autumn, 1987.

Hitchcock, A. S. *Manual of the Grasses of the United States, Volumes One and Two.* New York: Dover Publications, Inc., 1971.

Holmes, W. H. "Stone Implements of the Potomac-Chesapeake Tidewater Province". *Fifteenth Annual Report of the Bureau of American Ethnology.* 1897.

Justice, Noel D. *Stone Age Spear and Arrow Points.* Bloomington: Indiana University Press, 1987.

Kalm, Peter. *Travels in North America.* New York: Dover Publications, Inc., 1987.

Klots, Alexander B. *A Field Guide to the Butterflies.* Boston: Houghton Mifflin, 1951.

Lincoff, Gary H. *The Audubon Society Field Guide to North American Mushrooms.* New York: Alfred A. Knopf, Inc., 1981.

Little, Elbert L. *The Audubon Society Field Guide to North American Trees.* New York: Alfred A. Knopf, Inc., 1980.

Martin, Alexander C. *Weeds.* New York: Western Publishing Company, 1972.

Martin, Alexander C., Herbert S. Zim, and Arnold L. Nelson. *American Wildlife and Plants.* New York: McGraw-Hill Book Company, 1951.

Marye, William B. "The Baltimore County Garrison." *Maryland Historical Magazine.* Vol. 16, 1921.

McClane, A. J. *McClane's Field Guide to Freshwater Fishes of North America.* Austin, Tex.: Holt, Rinehart, and Winston, 1965.

Mitchell, Robert T., and Herbert S. Zim. *Butterflies and Moths.* New York: Western Publishing Company, 1962.

Mittenthal, Suzanne Meyer. *The Baltimore Trail Book.* Baltimore, Md.: Johns Hopkins University Press, 1983.

Mountains to Marshes: The Nature Conservancy Preserves of Maryland. Maryland Chapter of the Nature Conservancy, 1991.

Newcomb, Lawrence. *Newcomb's Wildflower Guide.* Boston: Little, Brown & Co., 1977.

Nobel, Edward. *Field Guide to the Grasses, Sedges, and Rushes of the United States.* New York: Dover Publications, Inc., 1977.

Ostrander, Charles, and Walter Price, Jr. *Minerals of Maryland.* Natural History Society of Maryland, 1940.

Pasture and Range Plants. Phillips Petroleum Company, 1963.

Peterson, Lee Allen. *Edible Wild Plants.* Boston: Houghton, Mifflin, 1977.

Peterson, Roger Tory. *A Field Guide to the Birds.* Boston: Houghton Mifflin, 1980.

Peterson, Roger Tory, and Margaret McKenny. *A Field Guide to Wildflowers.* Boston: Houghton Mifflin, 1968.

Petrides, George A. *A Field Guide to Trees and Shrubs.* Boston: Houghton Mifflin, 1958.

Pough, Frederick H. *A Field Guide to Rocks and Minerals.* Boston: Houghton Mifflin, 1953.

Rafinesque, C. S. *A Life of Travels.* 1836.

Reed, Clyde F. *Floras of the Serpentine Formations of Eastern North America.* Reed Herbarium, 1986.

Reed, Clyde F. *The Ferns and Fern Allies of Maryland and Delaware, Including District of Columbia.* Reed Herbarium, 1953.

Reid, George K. *Pond Life.* New York: Western Publishing Company, 1967.

Rodale, J. I. *The Encyclopedia of Organic Gardening.* Emmaus, Pa.: Rodale Press, 1959.

Shuttleworth, Floyd S., and Herbert S. Zim. *Non-Flowering Plants.* New York: Western Publishing Company, 1967.

"Soldiers Delight—Historical Reminiscences." *Maryland Monthly Magazine.* Vol. 1, No. 5, 1906.

Spencer, Edward. "Soldiers Delight Hundred in Baltimore County." *Maryland Historical Magazine.* Vol. 1, 1906.

Stokes, Donald W. *A Guide to Nature in Winter*. Boston: Little, Brown, 1976.

Swain, Su Zan Noguchi. *Plants of Woodland and Wayside*. Garden City, N. Y.: Garden City Books, 1958.

Thoreau, Henry D. *The Journals of Henry D. Thoreau, Vols. 8–14*. New York: Dover Publications, Inc., 1962.

Wormington, H. M. *Ancient Man in North America*. Denver Museum of Natural History, 1957.

Index

Alternative common names appear within parentheses.

Bryum reedii, 116
Bulrush, 187
Bush-clover. *See Lespedeza*

Calocera, clammy, 180
Calocera viscosa, 180
Cardinal flower, 163
Carya, species, 135
Carya: cordiformis, 135; *ovata*, 135;
    tomentosa, 135
Cassia fasciculata, 131
Castanea: dentata, 136; *mollissima*, 171;
    pumila, 136
Cattail, common, 146, 147, 185, 219
Cedar, 6; eastern red, 199, 203
Celastris scandens, 97
Cerastium arvense var. *villosissimum*, 78
Cerastium arvense var. *villosum*, 73, 78
Cercis canadensis, 57
Chanterelle waxy cap, 108
Cherry, 194; black, 59, 126, 142; eastern
    dwarf, 103; sour, 103
Chestnut, 219; American, 100, 136; Chi-
    nese, 171, 175, 185
Chickweed, 79; extra hairy field, 78; ser-
    pentine (hairy field), 73, 78, 93, 212
Chicory, 122, 124, 142
Chimaphila: maculata, 131; *umbellata*, 131
Chinkapin, Allegheny, 136
Cichorium intybus, 122
Cinquefoil, dwarf, 116–17
Cladonia, species, 17, 18
Cladonia: cristatella, 18; *pyxidata*, 18
Claytonia virginica, 60
Commelina communis, 163
Compositae, family, 93
Convolvulus arvensis, 124
Cornus florida, 59
Creeper, Virginia, 171, 176
Crotalaria sagittalis, 140
Cyperaceae, 127–28
Cyperus species, 163
Cypripedium acaule, 74

Dactylis glomerata, 135
Daisy, 93
Daucus carota, 100
Dayflower, Asiatic, 163
Deerberry, 105
Dennstaedtia punctilobula, 135
Dentaria heterophylla, 67
Deptford pink, 93, 94, 100
Deschampsia caespitosa, 148
Desmodium: ciliare, 139; *cuspidatum*,
    139; *lineatum*, 139; *nudiflorum*, 136;
    rigidum, 139
Dianthus armeria, 93
Dicranum species, 115–16
Dogwood, flowering, 59, 74, 76, 163, 176,
    181, 188, 194
Dyospyros virginia, 125

Elaeagnus umbella, 74–75
Eleocharis species, 126
Epigaea repens, 74
Equisetum, 67
Eupatorium, species, 116, 139
Eupatorium: perfoliatum, 157; *rugosum*,
    157
Evening-primrose, 93

False Solomon's-seal, 143
Fameflower, 92 fig., 95, 124, 136, 142
Fern, 151; Christmas, 135, 142, 143, 192,
    206 fig., 207; hay-scented, 135, 142,
    143, 181; sensitive, 142
Festuca species, 148
Fimbristylis annua, 146
Fimbry, annual, 146
Flax, grooved yellow, 142
Fontinalis species, 127
Foxtail, green (bristlegrass), 157, 164
Funaria, species, 115–16
Fungi, 151, 180, 217–18

Gamagrass, eastern, 124
Gaylussacia baccata, 105

Milkwort, whorled, 131
Mimulus ringens, 134
Mint, 93, 96
Mocassin flower (pink lady's slipper), 74
Monarda fistulosa, 124
Monkey-flower, square-stemmed, 134
Moss, 16, 18, 44, 47, 115, 123, 128, 177, 192; broom, 115–16; peat, 168; sphagnum, 190 fig.; water, common, 127; white cushion, 115
Moss, broom, 115–16
Moss, club: tree, 67–68
Moss, cord, 115–16
Moss phlox (moss-pink), 72 fig., 73, 78–79, 128, 141–42, 166
Moss-pink. *See* moss phlox
Mullein, common, 171
Mushroom, 169; amanita, 165, 169; polypore, 181

Nyssa sylvatica, 135

Oak, 43–44, 59, 94, 105, 127, 156, 178, 212; blackjack, 102, 105, 166, 177, 201; chestnut, 136, 151–52, 177, 201; northern red, 143, 181, 192; post, 105, 177, 201; scrub (bear), 105
Oenothera species, 93–94
Oleaster. *See* olive, autumn
Olive, autumn (oleaster), 74–75, 194
Onoclea sensibilis, 142
Orchis, showy, 76
Orchis spectablis, 76

Parmelia species, 17, 18, 191
Parthenocissus quinquefolia, 171
Partridge-pea, large-flowered, 131, 139, 157
Path rush, 187
Pea, everlasting, 94
Persimmon, 125, 181
Phlox subulata, 73

Phytolacca americana, 135
Pine, 6, 15, 19, 27, 132; pitch, 106, 107, 199, 214–15; table mountain, 107, 214; Virginia (scrub), 15, 19, 47, 59, 103, 106–07, 184, 194
Pink lady's slipper. *See* mocassin flower
Pinus: pungens, 107; *rigida,* 106; *virginiana,* 15
Pipsissewa, 131
Plantain, downy rattlesnake, 111
Platanus occidentalis, 27–28
Pokeweed, 135, 188, 196
Polygala verticillata, 131
Polygonum, species, 135
Polygonum tenue, 158
Polyporaceae, family, 181
Polypore, milk-white toothed, 39
Polystichum acrostichoides, 135
Poplar, yellow. *See* tulip-tree
Populus: grandidentata, 76; *tremuloides,* 76
Potentilla canadensis, 117
Poverty grass. *See* three-awn
Prunella vulgaris, 93
Prunus: cerasus, 103; *serotina,* 59; *susquehanae,* 103
Puffball, gem-studded, 178, 179
Purpletop, 157
Pussytoes, plantain-leaved, 74
Pyrus Malus. See apple, common
Pyxie cup (goblet lichen), 18, 139, 142

Queen Anne's lace, 100, 124, 139, 142
Quercus: ilicifolia, 105; *marilandica,* 102; *prinus,* 136; *rubra,* 143; *stellata,* 105

Ragwort, small's, 95, 100
Raspberry, wine. *See* wineberry
Rattlebox, 140
Redbud, eastern, 57
Rhus radicans, 125–26
Rhus typhina. See sumac, staghorn
Robinia pseudo-acacia, 126

75, 111; ovate-leaved, 74; yellow, 69, 75

Vitis, species, 97

Walnut, black, 135, 194, 195
Willow, prairie dwarf, 103
Wineberry (wine raspberry), 124–25
Wintergreen, spotted, 131
Witch-hazel, 192

FAUNA

Accipiter, 151
Achorutes nivicolus, 53
Aeshna verticalis, 65
Agelenidae, family, 161
Agkistrodon contortrix, 109–10
Ant, mound-building, 74, 89, 97, 107, 196
Apis mellifera, 75

Bass, 11; largemouth, 87, 133, 147; small-mouth, 134; striped (rockfish), 86–87
Bear, black, 29, 30
Beaver, 24 fig., 26, 39, 40, 41, 63, 86, 87, 133
Beetle: carrion 97–98; darkling, 107–08; green tiger, 134–35; Japanese, 134; whirligig, 128
Bluebird, eastern, 45, 125, 162, 191, 215
Bluegill, 11, 146–47
Blue jay, 33, 150, 157, 165, 178
Bobcat, 209
Bobolink, 59
Bobwhite, northern, 59
Buckeye, 157
Bufo americanus, 49–50
Bunting, indigo, 104
Butterfly: monarch, 125; painted lady, 64–65; tiger swallowtail, 133, 138 fig., 140–41

Caddisfly, northern, 146
Calopteryx maculata, 97
Cambarus bartoni, 111
Cardinal, northern, 97, 100, 130, 179, 215
Carp, 133
Catbird, gray, 130, 145
Celastrina argiolus, 111
Cercyonis pegala, 107
Chelydra serpentina, 102
Chickadee, Carolina, 9, 28, 127, 130, 204, 208, 215, 219, 220
Chuck-will's-widow, 81
Cicada, 122, 127, 130; annual (dogday harvestfly), 106; periodical, 88–89
Cinindela, species, 134–35
Clinostomus funduloides, 131
Coenagrionidae, family, 100
Common blue, 111
Copperhead, northern, 92 fig., 109
Corydalus, species, 97
Cottontail, eastern, 100
Cottus bairdi, 99
Cougar, 209, 210, 211
Cowbird, brown-headed, 67
Coyote, 206 fig., 208–09
Crayfish, eastern, 111, 151, 178
Crescent, pearly, 157
Cricket, field, 100, 122, 130, 176, 178, 184, 201
Crossbill, red, 4 fig., 15
Crow, American, 33, 68, 130, 165, 178, 203, 212, 215
Cuckoo, 67; black-billed, 75–76; yellow-billed, 134, 138 fig., 151, 180
Cynipinae, family, 102
Cyprinus carpio, 133

Dace, 97, 128; blacknose, 131; rosyside, 131
Damselfly, 115; black-winged, 97, 126, 127; narrow-winged, 100
Darner, eastern blue, 65

About the author

Jack Wennerstrom is a freelance writer and naturalist who lives in Randallstown, Maryland.

Soldiers Delight Journal was composed in Adobe Minion with Poetica display type on a Macintosh and designed by Kachergis Book Design, Pittsboro, North Carolina; and printed and bound by BookCrafters, Chelsea, Michigan.